Life: You're Doing It Wrong

Why People Don't get Better Results from Self-Improvement...
And What To Do About It!

By

Robert Manis, PhD

Copyright 2014 by Robert Manis
All rights reserved under International and Pan-American Copyright Conventions. Published in the United States by Modern Perspectives Press, Charleston Heights, Nevada, 89107
Library of Congress Cataloguing-in-Publication Data
Manis, Robert, 1952-
Life - you're doing it wrong: why positive thinking, therapy and spirituality don't always work - and what does - Modern Perspectives Press
Library of Congress Number 2013900765
ISBN: 9781625901811
Manufactured in the United States

DEDICATION

To Jagadish

Wisdom is the principal thing; therefore get wisdom: and with all your getting, get understanding.

(Proverbs 4:7)

TABLE OF CONTENTS

Prologue—Out of the Eclipse ... ix

Chapter One—Thoughts, Feelings and the Pursuit of Happiness ... 1

Chapter Two—Rethinking Happiness and Unhappiness ... 21

Chapter Three—The Motion of Emotions ... 47

Chapter Four—The Unconscious Mind ... 65

Chapter Five—Turning East ... 83

Chapter Six—The New Age ... 111

Chapter Seven—The Meaning of Life ... 135

Chapter Eight—Putting *Most of It* Together ... 159

Acknowledgments ... 177

Appendix—Recommended Reading, Endnotes, and Further References by Chapter ... 179

About the Author ... 187

Prologue

OUT OF THE ECLIPSE

The evening shadows fell long on the deserted highway as I drove through desolate western Nevada, approaching Carson City just as night was falling. After some confusion navigating the unfamiliar town, I found my destination, a historic downtown hotel, and checked into my room on the second floor. I was on the last leg of my travels through the Southwest, a trip I'd undertaken during a period of depression and much soul-searching.

I wasn't hungry, so I turned on the TV to kill an hour before venturing out to look for a place for dinner. Clicking around with the remote for a few minutes, I landed on the History Channel and a show about the development of Albert Einstein's Theory of General Relativity. Almost immediately, I was hooked. It seems that after Einstein came up with his theory, the challenge was to design an experiment to prove it. Although his Theory of Special Relativity, which related to particles, was by then widely accepted, General Relativity had some remarkable implications that were highly controversial and astounding. Two of these were that time itself moved more slowly at higher speeds and that space itself was literally warped or curved by gravity's force.

After a long correspondence, Einstein and a British astronomer named Arthur Eddington came up with a workable experiment to test the theory that space was curved. They postulated that one could observe the light coming from the stars during a solar eclipse and measure whether the sun's huge gravitational field bent that light. It was a reasonable experiment, and astronomers from around the world clamored to put together expeditions to the sites of future eclipses to test Einstein's theory.

Unfortunately, many problems, including cloudy weather, World War I, a mathematical error on Einstein's part, and flaws in telescope lenses of the time caused the proof to be delayed for over a decade. For starters, the outbreak of war prevented any communication between Einstein and Eddington, who each lived in a nation at war with the other, Germany and England. A group of astronomers who were ready to measure an eclipse lost their window when they were taken as prisoners of war in Eastern Europe, and Eddington himself was nearly imprisoned in England as a conscientious objector to the war. Further, an observation in California turned out to be flawed and several others were washed out due to the weather.

In 1919, after the war ended, Eddington got his final chance and sent two expeditions to different countries along the line of the ecliptic in hopes of getting a clear view. The eclipse would be directly in front of the Hyades star cluster that appears in the constellation Taurus, providing an unusually accurate way of gauging the displacement of light. In one of the locations, the view was largely clouded, and in the other, Eddington had focused the telescope the night before without taking into account the change in the next day's temperature. Fortunately, his backup telescope provided clear enough photos to do the analysis, and the data supported Einstein's prediction of how much the stars' position was bent by gravity. In the end, the delays proved fortunate, giving Einstein time to correct a major error in his mathematics, so that Eddington's results were close enough to match and prove the now famous Theory of Relativity.

My hunger finally won out over Einstein, and I stepped out to find a restaurant for some dinner. It was dark as I walked down the main street of Carson City, my way lit by a rising moon, and in my mind I continued to mull over what I had just seen on TV. I was struck by the role of luck and imagination, in addition to scientific reasoning and hard work, that Einstein's discovery entailed. But another thought started to slowly formulate in my mind, as I recalled the many images of solar eclipses repeatedly shown on the screen throughout the TV program.

Isn't it interesting, I suddenly realized, that the moon is the *exact* right size—neither too big nor too small—to almost totally block out the orb of the sun as it is viewed from the earth's perspective? I asked myself, can this be the case for all planets in solar systems throughout the universe? As I thought about it logically, the answer was obviously no. The moon, or moons, of a planet will orbit at various distances from it, and every planet is a different distance from its sun. Some moons would appear to more than block out the sun in their solar system and others would fail to completely block it. How odd is it that the earth has a single moon that almost *exactly* blocks the sun?

As I pondered this, I had what might be called a religious moment. It seemed as if the Creator had made the two spheres in exactly the right proportion to show that there was something special about life on earth. It was symbolic. And then I started to think, well, if it really is symbolic, then what precisely did the symbolism mean? I pondered this matter for some time, but it wasn't until a few days later that the meaning—for me, at least—became clear.

Symbolically, I decided, this perfect fit of moon over sun could mean that the light of knowledge was completely blocked out by the shadow of ignorance, a reflection of the condition of life on planet earth. On the bright side, though, I noted that the light from the sun wasn't *more* than blocked out—little bits of light bled around the circumference during a full eclipse. Even though the darkness of ignorance blocked the light, it was not enough to prevent the outline of truth from being discerned.

This realization gave me hope. I had just gone through a dark period in my life, in which I had come to question the beliefs and experiences I'd depended on over the course of my lifetime. But there was something else I pondered with this realization. Why was it, I wondered, that I had never noticed this before, and even more strange, why had no one else ever mentioned this odd coincidence about solar eclipses? Being a sociologist by profession, I knew that people have a tendency to ignore the obvious, but this seemed too startling a phenomenon to go so unremarked. Hadn't people being looking at the sky and asking questions since the dawn of time?

It was in the midst of this inquiry about the universe and the meaning of life on earth that I resolved to look with fresh eyes on all the world's knowledge. If something as significant as the moon and sun's ecliptic "fit" had been overlooked by humankind, then I would have to come to my own conclusions about all such important matters, regardless of what those conclusions might be. The very nature of "knowledge" deserved my scrutiny, as I could no longer rely on assumptions that everything was all figured out. I began to question what it is we know and how we know it.

Here's a little bit about my background that might explain my decision to take this new direction. I have a Ph.D. in sociology, but my interests have been far-ranging. I set out in my career by first majoring in criminology, but a course on deviance persuaded me that what is normal is just as problematic as what isn't. That led me to study the sociology of knowledge for my master's degree. But that in turn led me into the sociology of religion as I began my doctorate, when I started to see how religions shaped our basic world view. I dropped out for a few years, and when I came back, my interests had moved to organizational sociology and finally to social psychology. I have taught courses in the psychology of dreams and have had a lifelong interest in spirituality and religion. I have also been involved in the therapeutic movement of co-counseling and experienced a number of years of individual psychotherapy. If my life has a coherent thread, it is my long-time interest in the questions of what we really know and how we know it.

This book is the result of the discoveries I made in following that interest. My inquiry brought me to some basic understandings about life and how we can best live it. Not surprisingly, that included questioning the traditional wisdom of psychology, spirituality, and the popular self-help movement as voiced by so many best-selling books consumed by readers today.

What follows is a gradual unearthing of a new solution that draws on many earlier approaches to not only finding happiness but reducing unhappiness. Reducing unhappiness, it turns out, is a more effective way to go about it, as it circumvents the often debilitating quandary expressed as, "Am I doing it right?" which all too often must be answered negatively as happiness languishes just out of grasp, but also perhaps just around the corner out of sight.

CHAPTER 1

THOUGHTS, FEELINGS, AND THE PURSUIT OF HAPPINESS

What *do* we really know? Not that much, if you ask the philosophers. In fact, I remember reading the Encyclopedia of Philosophy entry on "knowledge" at the beginning of my masters' degree program, and there were more than a dozen pages just debating what the term itself means. Even Descartes' famous dictum, *I think therefore I am*, has been criticized, though perhaps unfairly.

But if we start with what we do know, it appears that apart from the validity of their actual content, we do know we have thoughts, and we also know we have feelings. Those thoughts and feelings may be based on something real or not, but it is clear that we have them.

It's not much, but it's something, and I think that even this fundamental observation, about having thoughts and feelings, simple as it is - remarkably has not been understood in its full significance for how best to live life as I will show in this book.

Furthermore, I would hope to clarify how we think about spirituality and psychology, starting with the fundamental observation that we have thoughts and feelings and asking several questions: How does the distinction between thoughts and feelings illuminate our understanding of ourselves and our lives? What is the relationship between thoughts and feelings? Do we really understand the significance of the relationship between the two? Which comes first? Just as there are thoughts about thoughts, aren't there feelings about feelings? Have we really paid enough attention to these simple facts?

And finally, how does all this relate to what people searching for happiness or self-improvement are implicitly asking, which is this: *Am I doing something (like my entire life!) wrong?* What so many self-help books inherently imply, I will argue, is *Yes*, you are.

In fact, regarding the last question, I believe the real answer is both yes and no. No, in that given what we understand, we are actually doing our absolute best. But *yes*, in that I think I've found some basic misunderstandings that permeate the popular mindset, ones that are only now starting to surface in our understanding of ourselves.

Unfortunately, these very same ones permeate the self-help books that attempt to help us and are based on the fact that not enough attention has been paid to the relationship between thoughts and feelings, and how they relate to our understanding of our circumstances, especially happiness. Now I am not totally against self-help books—I think they are useful in helping people to gain new ideas—but most are based on very basic misunderstandings about how to apply the help they offer.

Logically, it is easy to see that aside from being simply thoughts and feelings, there are four possible ways in which thoughts and feelings can combine: thoughts about thoughts, feeling about thoughts, thoughts about feelings, and feelings about feelings. Examples of these might be: I have a thought about you the reader. I also may have a feeling of nervousness about that thought, for example, *Will you like this book?* I then likely would have a thought questioning whether it was appropriate to share that feeling. Finally, I might feel embarrassed about the feeling of nervousness. Thoughts about thoughts have been dubbed *reflexive thoughts* and we could make a similar label of *reflexive feelings*.

Keep all this in mind as we go through our discussion, because this deeper understanding of thoughts and feelings is a cornerstone of our exploration and will be important in understanding my approach to achieving happiness. I will attempt to show that happiness is the result of a fusion of the two types of internal activity mentioned—a *feeling* about a *thought*.

How we put together our specific thoughts and feelings is the important thing, however, and requires us to go into a little detail and description about what happiness is, how our various types of thoughts and feelings operate, and how their effects upon us play out.

HAPPINESS: A NATURAL RIGHT?

The pursuit of happiness is such a fundamental activity for us humans (aside from the human struggle for survival), that it is enshrined in our nation's Declaration of Independence as a human right. We can thank Thomas Jefferson for including this in his careful wording of the draft that, after some revising by Benjamin Franklin and others, became our country's most important document.

By all reports, the crafter of the Declaration of Independence was not only a brilliant man, but a temperamental one. Madly in love with his beautiful wife, Jefferson became despondent over her death at age 33. He withdrew to his home at Monticello and refused to answer the many calls to service in his new government.

Believing him to be suicidal, his friend John Adams and others maneuvered his appointment to the ambassadorship of France where they hoped Paris— the City of Light —would cheer him up. But not long after his arrival, his youngest daughter Lucy died in America of whooping cough, and he was again plunged into deep depression. It wasn't until the young slave Sally Hemmings accompanied his other daughter to Paris and allegedly became his mistress that he recovered.

Appointed afterwards by George Washington to be Secretary of State, Jefferson feuded with Alexander Hamilton to such a degree that Washington requested his resignation and never spoke to him again. Four years later, as an opposition party Vice-President under John Adams, Jefferson engaged in a secret campaign with the French to undermine the Adams administration, trying to incite the French to invade England. And finally as President, he made it his mission to completely destroy the opposing Federalist party, which he succeeded at doing.

Fortunately for us, Jefferson's emotionality probably made him into the great writer he was, and of course, he had Ben Franklin to help him out. Most scholars believe that Jefferson's famous line in the Declaration about our inalienable rights to life, liberty, and the pursuit of happiness can be traced to his study of the English philosopher John Locke with a little editing by Franklin.

Whether the encoding of happiness for the first time in a nation's charter had any influence on its subsequent culture is subject to debate, but it is clear that in the 21st century, people in America are far more interested in happiness than in duty, honor, faith or virtue, or any of the other ideals of the 18th Century.

And that may even be a good thing - but it hasn't led to the results you might think.

SEEKING HAPPINESS

Right now books about happiness are extremely popular. A search on Amazon finds over 21,000 titles, including *The Happiness Advantage: The Seven Principles of Positive Psychology; The Happiness Hypothesis: Finding Modern Truth in Ancient Wisdom; The How of Happiness: A New Approach to Getting the Life You Want; Delivering Happiness: A Path to Profits, Passion, and Purpose; Authentic Happiness:*

Using the New Positive Psychology to Realize Your Potential; The Art of Happiness, 10th Anniversary Edition: A Handbook for Living; Happiness: A Guide to Developing Life's Most Important Skill, and many more. Apparently, happiness is such a good thing it even helps pay the bills, not that many people need to be convinced.

At the same time, there is evidence of the beginning of a dark countercurrent in this happiness deluge, with books having such titles as: *The Happiness Trap: How to Stop Struggling and Start Living* by Dr. Russ Harris and *Bright-Sided: How Positive Thinking Is Undermining America* by Barbara Ehrenreich. But whatever the case, it is clear that despite reading many books about happiness, Americans remain essentially no happier - at least, according to the Gallup Poll which polls daily on the subject and typically finds that happiness correlates highly with economic circumstances *not* with quantity of self-help books read.

In fact, it may be that these books have had the *opposite* effect. Psychologist Todd Kashdan wrote in 2010 of a surprising study that found those who'd just read a fake article on the "science of happiness" were less likely to enjoy events in their environment than people who'd read the same article where the word happiness was replaced by "accurate judgements."

Not surprising, though, to the author of one of the very first books on happiness, the legendary Alan Watts, whose first bestseller in 1940 was entitled *The Meaning of Happiness*. While I haven't read many of the more recent books on happiness, I did read Watts, who begins with a paradox that the more recent authors seem largely unaware of, that, in his own words, "those who seek happiness, do not find it."

This important observation takes Watts on a long exploration through Jungian psychology and Eastern philosophy which, while fascinating and highly influential in foreshadowing both the humanistic psychology and New Age spirituality movements, is now mostly forgotten. Perhaps, as it turns out, his exploration was a bit of a dead end, in that neither movement has progressed much further in the last 70 years.

But his argument that those who seek happiness, do not find it, rings true today as a reminder that self-help and self improvement books pointing people in one direction are really doing the opposite, albeit unintentionally. In Buddhist understanding, grasping and reaching for something are the very actions that prevent any real satisfaction. But worse, their same critique can be leveled against their own desired emotional states, like contentment, peace, compassion. The more you strive, it seems, the further you become from your goal.

What I intend in my exploration of happiness is to go down a slightly different path than Watts. My aim is to precisely explain the circumstances under which happiness arises, *why* happiness generally eludes those who pursue it, and what can be done to reduce unhappiness.

In a way, my work parallels some of the recent writings on Buddhism and happiness, but from a different perspective and minus the Buddhist terminology and philosophy that prevents it from being usable by a wide range of people - in essence refereeing in the debate between seeking happiness and the more circumspect Buddhist perspective.

All of this ties into my earlier mention of thoughts and feelings, and how a deeper understanding of their nature sheds light on happiness and unhappiness. My general view is that people are the way they are, and reforming or changing them is often doomed to backfire, so let us deal with what we have. We know we can't change other people, but that's often unclear how much we can change when it comes to ourselves. I will present some insights of psychology that underscore how difficult it is to change ourselves in any deep and meaningful way.

Of course, it is possible to change our behavior through motivation, effort and training, but it is much more difficult to change our thoughts and even more difficult to change our feelings, the two being at the very core of our psychology. And unfortunately, also at the core of our happiness. Most books on self-improvement point us in the direction of attempting to change thoughts and feelings which I believe is their greatest weakness. In essence, they are telling us that we are doing life *wrong*, and if only we follow a new directive, will we do it right. Hence the title of this book.

However, instead of removing or somehow miraculously transforming our feelings and thoughts, and in the process perhaps invalidating our entire lives, what I propose is something different. I propose a new understanding of how we work interiorly—our *inner workings*—one that reduces conflict and changes the way we think about our feelings, and in that way produces a better result.

Evidently, neither therapy nor spirituality have been fully successful to this end. In 2010, the *New York Times* published a series of articles reviewing progress in the field of psychotherapy, and one of these, "My Life in Therapy" by Daphne Merkin, concluded that there is little evidence that major changes in personality happens even after decades of psychoanalysis. Likewise, I recall reading a biographical article in *Newsweek* in 2009 about Huston Smith, the religious scholar and author of the immensely respected book, *The World's Religions*. At 90, after a lifetime of meditation and prayer, and even dropping acid, Smith is still trying to quiet his mind.

I can personally attest to the difficulties of finding inner peace myself. In addition to obtaining a Ph.D. in sociology, I learned meditation at age 21 and have practiced ever since, at times in intensive contexts with a number of spiritual teachers. I also did five years of intensive therapy and a number of years of less intensive psychological work, only to find myself at age 57 in that motel room in Carson City questioning what I *really* knew—if anything. My point is not to devalue psychotherapy or spirituality, only to revisit them with the intention of understanding their proper role.

RETHINKING POSITIVE THINKING

The good news is that I have found there are some major missing pieces, which, when put together, allow a person to understand him or herself and get out of the self-improvement trap once and for all.

I emphatically want to clarify, however, that I am not going to the other extreme of saying you should just try to accept yourself the way you are, because that, too, is actually the same thing—*trying* to change your thoughts and feelings. Rather, what I intend is to show you a real and possible way out of the trap of trying, which is through understanding better how we humans all work.

Yoda says in *Star Wars*, "There is no try, just do." But when it comes to the mind, things actually aren't so simple. If they were so simple, we could just buy one positive thinking book and be done with it! Sadly, not so. While it is well known and well-proven that happy thoughts produce endorphins and other body chemicals that are healthy and happiness-sustaining, and unhappiness produces stress hormones like cortisol and ACTH to inhibit body function, it has *not* been proven that *trying* to be happy has the same results.

In fact, I believe that *trying to be happy* is likely to produce much the same physical results as *being* unhappy, while expressing and accepting one's unhappiness in the right manner, if one can, produces many positive physical effects. While this has not yet been empirically proven, there are good reasons to think it is so.

Both suppression of negative thoughts and application of positive thoughts can tend to backfire, as Harvard social psychologist Daniel Wegner has shown in his research. Wegner calls the first item *thought suppression,* or the "White Bear hypothesis," after its original source in Tolstoy, where the author convinces his brother to try *not* to think of a white bear for a short time. Of course, he is then unable to banish the thought from his mind. Nowadays, we know of this as the "Try not to think of an elephant" conundrum. Wegner performed a series of experiments in which he confirmed that various kinds of attempts at thought suppression not only failed, but produced the opposite of the intended result, which is obsessive thinking. Instead of suppression of thought, distraction or even rumination directly on the subject produced better results.

Wegner's research has been validated by several other researchers. Joanne Wood and others of the University of Waterloo in

Ontario, Canada, found that people with low self-esteem especially have problems with positive thinking. She looked at the effectiveness of positive affirmations (e.g. *I'm lovable*) on people with both high and low self-esteem, and found that volunteers with low self-esteem actually felt worse after repeating the affirmation. She theorized that repeating sweeping positive self-statements, such as *I'm lovable,* makes people with low self-esteem think contradictory thoughts, such as *I'm not as lovable as I could be,* and it made those subjects feel even worse when contradictory thoughts persisted in breaking through.

Wood's study did not totally refute positive thinking. Participants with high self-esteem did benefit some from repeating *I'm lovable.* In the end, she concluded, "Repeating positive self-statements may benefit certain people, but backfire for the very people who 'need' them the most."

Similarly, Gerald Haeffel of Notre Dame University found the same kind of backfire effect with certain kinds of students when he studied how college students at risk for depression responded to positive thinking workbooks designed to prevent the mood disorder. Students of the personality type known as ruminators, who repetitively focus on the consequences and causes of negative moods, had dramatically worse symptoms of depression after completing the workbook as compared to similar students who received other types of workbooks. Again, as with Wood, Haiffel seems to have found that positive thinking is most likely to backfire with those who would seem to need it most.

Even uplifting music was found to backfire with certain types of people. Psychologists Myriam Mongrain and Susan Sergeant looked at the effects of gratitude exercises and listening to music on people classified as either self-critical or needy. While both activities seemed to have some benefit for the self-critical people, neither activity worked with those classified as needy and, in fact, both made them feel worse. The researchers hypothesized that this was probably because the activities didn't address the subjects' real issues.

I need to take a moment here to say a few words about our judgments about these types of people. We seem to have very strong value judgments against complainers, whiners and needy people which stem, I believe, from our reactions and responses to our own similar tendencies and feelings. Needy and critical people tend to get rejected by other people who feel uncomfortable or put on the spot by those feelings. We tend to submerge our own experience of rejection until someone brings it up by being needy or self-critical, and then we react against them, thus completing a vicious cycle.

What I have found is that both groups need more empathy, which is precisely what they do not get. (But don't hold your breath trying to empathize in order to change them!) I have had friends ask me, "How can you put up with me, when I feel this way?" My response has always been, "If I can't be with you, I know it's only because I can't be with some part of myself."

IRONIC PROCESSES

Wegner later discovered that the failure of thought suppression was a specific example of what he called, in a larger sense, "ironic processes," or mental actions that produce results opposite of their intention. He hypothesized that two different mental processes were responsible for this effect: the first, an "operating" process that tries to accomplish something; and second, a "monitoring" process that then looks for contrary evidence regarding that accomplishment. Under normal circumstances, the two work in harmony, but under stress, the "monitoring" process becomes dominant because it is cognitively less taxing, actually producing an outcome contrary to what was originally intended.

How can this be? For an answer, it is necessary to better understand not just the workings of the human mind, but the purpose and function of it as well. It is the basic assumption of my argument that *humans are designed to try to survive, and most features of human structure are at least minimally functional in that regard.* Note that I am not saying *optimal*. Rather, just enough to get by. I don't think that this assumption is stretching things too much, because despite the efforts of nature and of humans' best efforts to kill each other off, we are still here after millions of years. Whether that continues, so far as I can tell, may well have to do with finding better ways than killing to keep humans occupied.

So it is likely that Wegner's ironic processes, like our emotions themselves as I will discuss in Chapter Three, is one of the many features that allows humans to survive, if not always to thrive. Fortunately, there are a couple of solutions to Wegner's dilemma which I will relate later in developing my overall thesis.

So having posed the basic question of how we find happiness (or lessen unhappiness) when the very attempt seems to be doomed and even counter-productive, we are almost ready to begin! But don't despair, I promise you there is a solution.

The way I intend to approach that solution will cover these questions and topics:

- Is there a basic "right way" to live?
- A definition and explanation of happiness
- Exploration of psychological aspects of happiness, including emotions and the unconscious
- Spirituality and its relationship to happiness
- How happiness relates to the meaning of life
- What is *paradoxical intention,* and its significance in reducing suffering and eliminating "trying" (Wegner's *ironic processes*)

What I will show you is that while *trying* to be happy—and indeed all forms of control—is doomed in most instances, the basics of successful living have been known since ancient times. With the help of these basics, plus the modern understanding of the emotions, the unconscious, the spiritual, and meaning-making processes of the mind—each of which is necessary *but not sufficient* for most people—unhappiness can be reduced, and the quality and meaning of life can be improved.

I will start off by introducing you to the world's first self-help book (and no, I don't mean the Bible), which will help us explore whether or not there is a right way to live. But then, things will start to get even more interesting after that.

A HANDBOOK FOR LIVING

Imagine a bright day in Rome around 70 AD. It's the reign of the Emperor Vespasian, the fourth ruler to lead Rome since the death of Nero two years earlier. Life has returned to normal as the Emperor, reputed to have divine powers, is consolidating his reign. The Stoic philosopher Musonius Rufus is holding court outside with his students, the only philosopher not banned by the Emperor, a fact that arouses much curiosity among the public.

A thin teen-aged boy, well-dressed but lame and clothed like a slave hovers around the outskirts of the group, propped up by a crutch.

"May I answer?" the boy requests after a difficult question by Rufus has silenced the group.

"What's your name, son?" the philosopher inquires kindly, silencing the laughter of his students.

"Epictetus, sir." The laughter breaks out again, this time over the boy's name which means in Greek "acquired," as given by a master too lazy to think of something more original.

"Who is your master?" Rufus asks, again quieting the laughter.

"Epaphrodites, sir," naming the late Nero's powerful secretary who was banished for helping the Emperor commit suicide. Some murmuring ensued, but Rufus once more quieted the throng.

"And what is the essence of my philosophy, young man?"

"To truly understand what is within one's power and to apply all one's strengths in that alone," the young man replied with a strong voice.

"That is better said than by anyone here, and maybe even by myself. You are welcome to join us," Rufus welcomed him into the fold with an embrace – (at least that's the way I imagine the scene).

I've used this imagined scenario to introduce you to the very first self-help book, one that was written nearly 2,000 years ago. It was given out by the young man I described who became another philosopher, one who felt, like Rufus, that philosophy was not just for other philosophers but for all people. I say "given out," because Epictetus, like many of his time, never wrote down their own words. Later, those words were transcribed by his own student, Arrian, and used to teach the Roman philosopher-king Marcus Aurelius.

The book is the *Enchiridion* by Epictetus, commonly translated as the *Manual* or *Handbook,* and most recently (1994) as *The Art of Living,* edited by Sharon Lebell.

The *Handbook*, as I prefer to call it, has been for many centuries a beacon for the philosophically minded, all the way through history down to modern times when it gave hope and support to a prisoner of war who made it back to tell his tale.

On September 9, 1965, Commander James Stockdale, a 42-year-old career aviator fatefully climbed into his A-4E Skyhawk fighter on the USS Oriskany off the coast of Vietnam. Minutes later, his plane disabled by friendly fire, he was forced to eject and parachuted into hostile North Vietnam where he was quickly surrounded, beaten and taken into custody. For the next seven years, he was tortured and beaten, kept in a 3'x 9' cell in leg irons with lights on day and night. He was mentally tortured as well by the fear that he would betray the knowledge of what he had personally witnessed a year before, that the Gulf of Tonkin incident which had led our nation into war was largely fabricated. When he was told he was going to be paraded in public for propaganda purposes, he deliberately cut his face to prevent his captors from doing so. Along with a dozen other resisters, he became known as a member of the "Alcatraz Gang," a group so troublesome to their captors, they were kept in solitary confinement as tight as the San Francisco Bay island prison for the last years of the war.

What kept him going throughout those years? He credited his survival partly to a book he read when the Navy had sent him to Stanford University for graduate work—the *Handbook* by Epictetus.

Epictetus himself was no stranger to life's ups and downs. He was born in the sacred city of Hierapolis, in Phrygia in modern Turkey, only to see the city leveled by a huge earthquake before reaching the age of ten. How he came to Rome and was maimed is not known, but some say his leg was broken by his master who, in his guilt, let the boy study freely and eventually gave him his freedom. It's not clear whether Epictetus ever saw his family again, but his owner was exiled and eventually executed, and his teacher Rufus exiled several times. He himself was exiled by the emperor Domitian in 93 AD and lived simply the last 30 years of his life, far from Rome.

The 93 dictums and their explanation contained in the *Handbook* are a pillar of clarity. I have many times read them out loud or over the phone to others who are invariably struck by its timeliness 2,000 years later. In fact, most people find it better and more concise than its more recent successors in the self-help realm. Its first insight is that happiness and freedom are in truly understanding what things are within our control to change and what things are not. Most simply, it says that events and other people are not within our control, but our actions and reactions are. I recommend people buy or download Epictetus' timeless tome and refer to it from time to time.

I remember a plaque on the wall in my uncle and aunt's house, what is now know as the Serenity Prayer, as formulated decades ago by the theologian Reinhold Niebuhr and spread around the world by the Alcoholics Anonymous organization:

God, grant me the serenity to accept the things I cannot change,
Courage to change the things I can,
And wisdom to know the difference.

I am not sure whether Niebuhr had read the *Handbook*, but many people think so, and Epictetus does precisely attempt to impart the wisdom to tell the difference between what can and cannot be changed. Perhaps it's a bit depressing to consider that 2,000 years later, few authors have been able to match his depth, but it is certainly clear that much about the human condition is still the same.

Nevertheless, in my opinion there is one thing that is fundamentally different about our understanding of life since then, and that is our post-Freudian appreciation of the complexities of the human psyche. It is that subtle but profound difference that perhaps can be amended to Epictetus's opus, which is what I would attempt, if I may humbly try.

In addition, I would also like to bring to the ancient wisdom some ideas that have been floating around the popular culture from the New Age and human potential movement, because they have something to say about the spiritual nature of the human being that during the previous eras of religious orthodoxy could not be said. Hopefully in all this, there is the potential for a real synthesis, a place where the pieces can fall together and fit in a way that makes sense—and in a way that makes Epictetus' advice easier to apply.

I include here several of Epictetus' principles, in the bullets below, to give you a taste. The following are from the classic (18th century) translation by Elizabeth Carter as appearing in Wikiquotes:

- Some things are in our control and others not. Things in our control are opinion, pursuit, desire, aversion, and, in a word, whatever are our own actions. Things not in our control are body, property, reputation, command, and, in one word, whatever are not our own actions.

- People are disturbed, not by things, but by the principles and notions which they form concerning things.

- It is the act of an ill-instructed man to blame others for his own bad condition; it is the act of one who has begun to be instructed, to lay the blame on himself; and of one whose instruction is completed, neither to blame another, nor himself.

- With every problem, ask yourself what abilities you have for making a proper use of it. If you see an attractive person, you will find that self-restraint is the ability you have against your desire. If you are in pain, you will find fortitude. If you hear unpleasant language, you will find patience. And thus habituated, the appearances of things will not hurry you away along with them.

- Remember that you ought to behave in life as you would at a banquet. As something is being passed around it comes to you; stretch out your hand, take a portion of it politely. It passes on; do not detain it. Or it has not come to you yet; do not project your desire to meet it, but wait until it comes in front of you. So act toward children, so toward a wife, so toward office, so toward wealth.

- Everything has two handles, the one by which it may be carried, the other by which it cannot. If your brother acts unjustly, don't lay hold on the action by the handle of his injustice, for by that it cannot be carried; but by the opposite, that he is your brother, that he was brought up with you; and thus you will lay hold on it, as it is to be carried.

- Instead of averting your eyes from the painful events of life, look at them squarely and contemplate them. By facing the realities of death, infirmity, loss and disappointment, you free yourself of illusions and false hopes, and avoid miserable and envious thoughts.

- Even death is no great concern in of itself. It is our notion of it, that it is terrible, that scares us. There are many ways to think about death. Ask yourself about death and everything else, whether your way of thinking about it helps you or hinders you.

- Assume that everything that happens, does so for some good ... Avoid jumping to conclusions, but ... think that all events contain an advantage for you if you look for them.

NOT SO FAST ....

One warning, though: Nowadays, the basic insight of Epictetus, regarding the difference between what we can control and what we cannot, is a little more problematic. In his day, one's body, status, health, and career were largely controlled by outside forces. He was a born a slave, later freed, and finally exiled by the Roman emperor.

But today, if you don't like your body or face, you can get plastic surgery. If your health is bad, take vitamins. Don't like your career? Go to a career counselor. Don't like the weather? Move to Hawaii. Even more complications occur when you factor in the self-help movement. There is literally nothing you aren't able to change according to one person or another. There are even seminars on physical immortality, where you allegedly can "free yourself from the culture of death" by purchasing a video for 40 bucks. So some common sense is needed. Maybe Reinhold Niebuhr made Epictetus' insight into the Serenity Prayer because he despaired over people not being able to figure it out anymore!

Fortunately, through "divine intervention," a timely chain email arrived in my inbox that gave me a handy, updated guide to what I can and cannot control. Listed under what I cannot control are the following:

1. Traffic (I can make choices about the route I take, but not the traffic I encounter.)
2. Weather
3. Airline Schedules (I can control having a book or cell phone, but not whether a flight is delayed.)
4. My In-laws, siblings, or parents
5. Other people's beliefs
6. Other people's attitudes
7. Other people's ethics
8. Other people's emotion
9. Other people's parenting
10. Other people's politics

I thought of a couple of others: World events and natural disasters. For most people, there's a few hours a week that can be saved by not worrying or grousing about these things. I know it's easy to worry about whether the weather will be good during your vacation, but aside from choosing the dates, there's not much you can do but take an umbrella... or snow shoes!

For all the rest of life, the question seems to be only how much time, energy, and money do you want to expend to try to solve the problem.

So, is that all there is to it? Not really, because those same "ironic processes" of Wegner that undermine positive thinking to sometimes produce the opposite effect, can undermine one's attempts at happiness through serenity as well.

But you will be glad to know that I have found some possible ways out of the self-improvement trap, a trap that not only prevents those who seek happiness from finding it, but also inhibits all those who want to improve themselves.

If you are a person that is trying to improve yourself, you no doubt have faced your repeated failures to achieve your ideals by rationalizing that you will "get there" to the place you seek eventually. The bad news is that you probably won't.

But the good news is that you actually don't need to. What follows is my attempt to show you that here is a different way to move forward and a different way to live your life. And that may be the most positive thing of all.

CHAPTER 2

RETHINKING HAPPINESS ... AND UNHAPPINESS

When I was in graduate school, one of my fellow teaching assistants liked to tell the following joke:

A professor is speaking to his class in a large lecture hall.

"My current research is exploring the link between sex and happiness, and I would like to do a survey of students in this class," he announces. "Will everyone who has sex *every day* please raise their hands?"

A group of students raise their hands. Looking at their smiling faces, it is obvious they are very happy.

"Good," the professor remarks. "Now would everyone who has sex *once a week* please raise their hands?"

A number of students raise their hands. Looking at them, it is obvious they are happy, too, but possibly not as happy as the first group.

"Great," he continues. "Now would everyone who has sex *once a month* raise their hands?"

A large number of students raise their hands. But they don't look very happy at all.

"Okay," the professor continues. "Now would everyone who has sex just *once a year* please raise their hands?"

One guy raises his hand. But he is smiling ear to ear. In fact, he looks even happier than the people who have sex every day.

"I don't understand." The professor hesitates. "You seem to disprove my research. Can you explain why you are so happy when you have sex only once a year?"

"Sure, doc," he responds. *"Today's* the day!"

Now this story contains much of what I will propose for understanding happiness, and actually illustrates my approach quite well. So let's get down to business and see where it takes us.

WHAT HAPPINESS IS AND ISN'T

There has been quite a bit of research in the last few years about happiness. Some studies show that positive thinking is correlated with happiness, others show that religiosity is related to happiness, as well as owning pets, gardening, getting exercise, having friends, helping others, watching less TV, making at least $70,000 a year (in 2010 dollars). In fact, there are quite a lot of things that are supposed to make people happier. The only thing I have *not* seen is that buying books on happiness makes people happier. In fact, judging from Alan Watts' observation that "those who pursue happiness, do not find it," I would bet that buying books on happiness could even make people less happy from the eventual disappointment.

I promise, though, that I will take special care to make sure this book does *not* do that. But how could all these promises be false, given that the information is based on scientific research? There are several reasons for this, but probably the biggest is that in scientific research, there is a principle that *correlation is not causation*. In other words, just because two things appear together does not mean that one causes the other.

To give you a couple of quick and obvious examples: Fire trucks do not cause fires, even though quite often, you see them *before* you see the fire. Ice cream does not cause rape, even though the total consumption of ice cream is related to the reported incidence of rape. In the first case, you may observe the effect before you see the cause. In the second case, there is a third variable—warmer temperatures—which causes a fourth variable— going outside— which together may cause the increased potential incidence of at least non-acquaintance rape. In neither case would eliminating fire trucks or ice cream be as effective as fireproofing buildings or getting rapists off the street.

Because correlation is not causation, it is likely that many of the studies we read about happiness are literally putting the cart before the horse—confusing the causes of happiness with their consequences. Happy people are more likely to have more friends, help others more, do constructive things like gardening or exercise, than depressed people. By the same token, people who are depressed may begin to doubt their faith, stop exercising, and stop doing any of the other healthy activities, as well as doing destructive things.

But none of that means if you are depressed, you will necessarily become happy if you do those healthy things. They may work for some people, of course, and I'd be the last one to say *not* to try them, but there are other methods available that are in fact quite surprising, methods that work even if you are lazy, and which, I think, may also have less chance of backfiring. By "backfire," I don't mean that helping others might make you more depressed (although conceivably it could), but rather that a depressed person might not be motivated to take a particular action, and so end up with one more thing to beat him or herself up about.

Now you may be thinking, *Tell me those other methods now!* And there is nothing I can do to keep you from skipping ahead to Chapter Seven where I do that – and you are welcome to! - but the truth is some of the techniques I propose are so simple and -I would say, downright *stupid*—that you might not believe them and so not use them in the proper way. In fact, I have to say that I'd discovered these methods for a year before I actually tried them even once, so convinced was I that they couldn't possibly work. I even considered titling this book *The Joke of Life*, because what I discovered seemed so ridiculous. So please, bear with me, and I will take you through to my discovery in a way that you will understand it fully and therefore be more convinced to apply it to your life.

But the short version of the path I will lead you along is this: Happiness is when you think you are getting what you want.

I repeat: Happiness is when you *think* you are getting what you want. That's why the student in my joke who answered, "Today's the day!" was happy, of course. The key is not that he actually did get laid, but that he *thought* he was going to get laid, which was what made him so happy. I am saying that it is not whether you actually get or don't get what you want, but the fact that you think you will, that is important. Even when you do actually get what you think you want, it may turn out to be not as good as you'd hoped, and of course, in the end you may not even get it. But in either scenario, you will be happy right up until the moment that you find out.

I discovered this simple truth about what makes us happy just *after* I'd defeated a month's long depression using the approach I'll tell you about in Chapter 7. Coming out of my depression, I shared the winning technique with a friend. He responded, "Have you ever thought about what happiness *really* is?" I replied, saying, like most people, that I hadn't, but I knew it when I saw it. He continued, offering his simple definition: "Happiness is when you get what you want."

I have to admit I recoiled when I first heard this, having a background in psychology, meditation, and personal growth, all designed to promote the notion that happiness ultimately comes from within, not from "out there." The thought that one could be happy by simply acquiring something was a bit materialistic and not very ennobling . But another part of me has learned to listen to views that are the opposite of my sacred beliefs and try to integrate them. After a moment, I responded, "I like it, even if it is pretty cynical."

I spent some time in the day afterwards pondering my friend's theory and found some obvious exceptions to it, which I am sure you can spot too. But then I realized that, as in most things, the key to a deeper understanding was not in the reality of it but in its perception. After all, most of what we experience is simply our perception of something rather than the objective truth of it.

For example, you may have had the experience of driving down a deserted highway and suddenly braking to avoid a wet spot, only to discover it was a reflection of the sky on the road. Likewise, you may have had the experience of walking down a trail at night and recoiled at the sight of a snake, only to discover it was actually a branch not a snake. What we react to is not the phenomenon itself, but its appearance – our perception of something—not necessarily its reality. Sociologists have their own version of this insight called the Thomas Theorem, which states, *What is believed to be real, has real consequences.* Philosophy has developed an entire school of thought based on the insight as well, called *phenomenology*.

It quickly became clear to me that happiness was *not* that we are getting what we want, as my friend had offered, but rather the *thought* or *belief* that we are getting what we want. That's right, the *thought* that we are getting what we want. The *reality* may not matter at all.

And there are some variations of that definition. Consider that the word *getting* is a verb. It exists in a present, past, and future version. In the present, while you are getting what you want, you think, *Yay, I am getting what I want!* In the past, after you got it, you think for a while, *Yay, I got what I want!* But the most important version is the future, because it is the version that potentially lasts the longest in time, *Yay, I am going to get what I want!* The anticipation can last minutes, hours, days, months, or occasionally even years, and because of this, the future is the version I want to mostly focus on for the rest of this book.

Staying in the future, there are also logical variations on this definition of happiness. These are:

- **Unhappiness** is when you think you are *not* going to get what you want.

- **Unhappiness** is when you think you are going to get what you *don't* want.

- **Happiness** is when you think you are *not* going to get what you *don't* want.

Examples of each follow, for when you think:

I am *not* going to get what I want: the job, girl or guy, house, whatever. (Unhappiness)

I am going to get what I *don't* want: sick, divorced, fired, whatever. (Unhappiness)

I am *not* going to get what I *don't* want,: sick, divorced, fired, whatever. (Happiness)

This is true for whatever the desired outcome is—whether you want to have sex, watch some TV, help others or even hurt them. You are happy if you think you will get the outcome you want or if you think you are performing a step in that direction, while you will be unhappy if you are blocked in that outcome. Likewise, you will be unhappy if you achieve an unwanted outcome or think you are going down that road, and happy if somehow that outcome is avoided. And so on.

When you reflect about it, that just about sums up the majority of most people's thoughts, at least during their free time! I'd be willing to wager that if you looked inside people's heads, you'd see a direct correlation between the thinking I've described and their happiness as experienced at a given moment.

Now it is also true that happiness can occur in the present or past tense: *I'm getting what I want, I got what I wanted,* or *I avoided what*

I didn't want. But as I said, the majority of these thoughts seem to occur about the future rather than the present. Additionally, in the present many of the desired outcomes don't turn out to be exactly what you may have wanted, or bring new concerns or desires that show up after the original desire was fulfilled. But you are happy thinking you were going to get what you wanted for a long period, right up until the point where you think, *Oh no, this wasn't what I expected!* Still, it is important to note that thoughts in the past, like *Yay, I got what I wanted*, or *I lived a full life*, do produce happiness, at least up until the next cycle of thoughts appear.

Some of you might object that you can have happiness while gazing at a flower. Nevertheless, in that example, the feeling follows from an outcome that people want—the enjoyment of beauty. (If they could have the same emotion from looking at dog excrement, I would be more impressed.)

You may also object that there are indeed transcendental states through which you could conceivably witness dog excrement with joy, during a religious or spiritual awakening, psychedelic drugs, or through divine love or *agape*, and I will agree with you. But note that those experiences are usually fleeting, and you may need my technique the rest of the time. Furthermore, such a transcendental experience may only increase your suffering if you are not careful of my point and keep trying to recreate the experience.

On the other hand, some might object that rich people can be unhappy, despite having everything they want. But my answer is that happiness is not in *having* something but in *getting* it. You've heard the saying, *Getting there is half the fun*, but sometimes it can be even more than half. Once something has been gotten, as everyone knows, the excitement begins to wear off. The malaise of the wealthy is easily understood. After getting everything they wanted, they become unhappy, because they realize that what they have isn't what they want after all, and may even be what they *don't* want.

Finally, you might object that this definition of happiness and its variations contradicts Epictetus, who essentially is saying in *The Handbook* that we can find happiness by understanding life, rather than by getting what we want. That would be untrue. Epictetus is telling us not to want things that are out of our control and to be philosophical about the rest. Following this advice produces serenity or contentment—if you can do it. But some people can't and then become frustrated in trying to live up to Epictetus' standard.

CONTENTMENT DOES NOT EQUAL HAPPINESS

Content people are typically happy but sometimes in a different way than we normally experience happiness. It is worth discussing contentment, however, because it actually holds a key for what I will present about my method later in Chapter Eight.

For most people, contentment is their experience when they get all or at least enough of what they want. They think, *I have got a good job, a good marriage, a good house, good health, and that is more than most people have.* We all know people who are like that. We also probably know others, who had all those things, but contentment wasn't enough for them, and so they had affairs, decided to look for a better job, questioned the meaning of life, or in some way rocked the boat in an attempt to get more.

From the point of view of contentment, these people perhaps made some big mistakes. If so, hopefully their mistakes were a learning experience, and that is valuable, too. But I would also, at least some of the time, beg to differ in seeing dissatisfaction as a problem, which is how Stoics and Buddhists see it. As I have tried to point out, the nature of happiness is transitory, and the nature of the mind, is, how shall I say... roving? Adventure-seeking? For many people a static life would be unfulfilling, even if it was, by outside appearances, a "good" one. It is simply not, after all, *what they wanted*! because of this, contentment is quite often a transitory state—just like happiness!

In any case, it is not my intention to write *The Seven Habits of Highly Contented People.* What works for them, might not work for you. Furthermore, I doubt whether it would be possible to improve on Epictetus in the realm he addresses. What I want to do, is give you a more complete landscape than he was able to. Then, rather than receiving a contentment "fish," you can learn to catch them on your own.

Finally, there is another form of contentment people find, which is more dynamic than what Epictetus is pointing to. That is the contentment that comes from being devoted to something larger than themselves. In that devotion to a cause or meaning, they may experience tremendous victories and catastrophic defeats, but somehow there is something that makes it all worthwhile. I will talk more about this as well in Chapter 7, because it has important implications, but for now it is enough to know that people are unique, and it is okay not being content—or not having any easy guide to achieving contentment.

COMPLAINTS AND CONGRATULATIONS

I've argued that what is most important about our thoughts is what they imply for the future, but that's not completely true. A very significant event happens at the moment you get or fail to get what you want. At that moment, you do one of two things. Depending on what happens you either congratulate yourself or complain to yourself. This has an immediate reinforcing effect on your state of mind. If you are congratulating yourself, you feel good in the same way you do when you are praised. If you do the opposite, complain, you feel bad. In essence, you are saying, *Yay, I did it right*, or *Oh no, I did it wrong...*

That particular thought creates a feeling of success or failure which may resound into the past or future as the thought hits up against your self-concept. When it does, you think whether you are a good person or not, and *then* your thoughts move into the future, about what may happen next. It is truly a significant moment that has a lot of personal impact.

Now, if you are afraid that I am here about to launch into a whole different kind of sermon about the virtue of praising yourself as positive thinking, you can relax. That is not exactly where I am going. But I think you can see now why positive thinking is so popular (at least among the non-depressed and non-ruminators amongst us), because it has an immediate effect on mood. In addition, positive thinking makes people happier in the medium term by stimulating the thought or fantasy that by using positive thinking they will be helped in getting what they want.

However, it's my belief, as well as Daniel Wegner's theory of ironic processes, that conventional positive thinking can be a double-edged sword, and in the long term as it is commonly practiced, could have a few detrimental effects. The easiest of these to see is that if a person *is* depressed, trying to think positively is just something to beat him or herself up about, as in: *What's the matter with me? Why can't I think more positively?*

As you may have noticed, those kinds of thoughts are a complaint, creating yet another burden of "doing it wrong." In a nutshell, the issue is this: When life serves you lemons, you are supposed to make lemonade. But sometimes you can't, at least for a while, and then you feel bad – doubly. You wish you could stop complaining (to yourself, because it doesn't matter psychologically whether you vocalize or internalize that complaint), and you end up complaining more.

But what if you congratulated yourself on these your natural reactions, even complaining? Now that would be some real positive thought! If life is made up of congratulations and complaints, once you can congratulate yourself on your complaints, you've got it made! That's a joke of course, but it is based on a very useful insight that parallels my technique as revealed in Chapter 7.

I recently saw a TV interview of a successful woman entrepreneur who was asked how she had come to be so innovative in her business. She replied that this ability came from her father, an inventor, who had congratulated her every time she failed. Like Thomas Edison, who famously failed a thousand times in his quest to develop the light bulb, her father believed every failure was a necessary step in eliminating what didn't work, and so worthy of praise. Through her father's approach, this woman had developed a similar way of turning her failures into a kind of success.

This kind of self-congratulation can work for your inner thoughts and feelings, as well. But I am not limiting its application to the moment of success or failure. Life contains a zillion moments, and this one simple trick will help you in a few of them, but perhaps not in all. In addition, what do you do if you end up having a feeling of disappointment from a failure, in spite of the congratulations? Suppress it? As Wegner points out, that may not work, causing instead the opposite of what you want, in keeping with his theory of ironic processes.

What if you did congratulate yourself on everything you were thinking and feeling, even those "bad feelings," such as disappointment.? Could you *really* do it if you were feeling bad in the first place? And if you could, wouldn't that be like rewarding yourself for bad behavior?

FEELING GOOD OR *DOING* GOOD?

One of the great misunderstandings of the self-help movement is that *feeling* good is the same as *doing* good. This misunderstanding may be due to the hijacking of Joseph Campbell's famous quote, in which he advises to "follow your bliss," often interpreted to mean that doing and feeling good can be one and the same.

Another confusion between feeling good and doing good happens when we are asked, *How are you doing?* and we respond with how we are feeling. *Fine, Not bad,* or *So-so,* we say. Rarely do we say, or hear someone say more honestly, *I'm feeling bad, but actually I am doing great.* While strange, that response would a least tell the full story, which is that we can be doing good while feeling bad. If you do dare to tell the honest truth that is anything less than "fine," you are immediately confronted with questions like, *Well, are you getting enough exercise?* or maybe advice like, *Oh, you should read this or that book …* What you don't get is probably what you needed most in the first place, a little empathy and understanding.

Doing well, of course, refers to the actions you are performing. These actions may or may not be having an immediate effect on your happiness, since happiness is usually dependent on the fulfillment of a want that is often out of your immediate control. Yet these actions may be important in that they are setting up your future ability to have what you want and avoid what you don't want, by improving your health or opportunities. Certainly Epictetus would have felt that a little self-discipline, while causing some discomfort in the present, would be "doing well" in producing a longer term happiness or contentment.

Working out provides some good examples of the truth I am getting at. While working out, you might feel tired, resentful, grumpy or just blah, but working out is healthy, so you're actually doing good but not feeling good. All athletes know the secret is to work out regardless of how you feel, and you will be "doing good." Alternatively, when working out, you may be feeling happy. This may sound like you're happy when doing the right thing, but it's not. Rather it is due to your expectations of a good result—what you think you will be getting, such as a buff body or reversal of obesity. But you are really only happy because the perception is at play, not because you are doing a "good" thing. Doing doesn't create feeling, but perception of doing can.

The reason you are happy when working out is you fantasize about what great shape you'll be in or the marathon you'll win. While it may not come true, it serves to motivate you to keep on working out. I hope my point is clear: Happiness is completely independent of how you are doing, coming from a completely different and independent emotional and mental mechanism. The myth that we can be happy because of what we're doing, rather than because our perception of what we are doing, (which is dependent on many things), is just not accurate.

Try it this way: Working out, you are not happy, but later when you are no longer obese, you are happy. Such happiness is due to *not getting what you don't want*, which is to be obese. But then consider what would happen if you wanted to get buff, but really, you just got a little less fat. Now you are unhappy, because you didn't get what you *did* want.

Because of this feeling good/doing well confusion, we can again see that while positive thinking as conventionally practiced may sometimes work to produce real happiness, it can work in producing the opposite. Because it makes you think you should be feeling good all of the time, positive thinking can be a set up for disappointment.

Positive thinking could also produce hypocrisy, in terms of people who won't say what they are really feeling. In general, positive thinking as practiced could easily tend to ignore reality for a sugary substitute, and people who don't deal with reality in the end rarely succeed for long.

For those of you who like positive thinking, and are still with me, don't put down the book. What I have to say will be far more positive than you might expect, but in a way that is more all-encompassing than you have been taught to practice. In order to understand my approach though, we are going to have to leave the world of thoughts and travel to the world of emotions. By way of entry, I would like to talk a little bit more about unhappiness, or as it is also known—*suffering*.

UNHAPPINESS AND SUFFERING

Aside from thinking you are not getting what you want, there are a few additional sources of unhappiness. If that were not the case, the last word on the subject would have been given 2,500 years ago by the Buddha's Four Noble Truths, the foundation of his teaching. The first two of these clearly state that: 1) life is inherently made up of suffering, and 2) our desires are the cause of that suffering.

You can see that the second is a simplified way of saying pretty much what I have been saying, in perhaps a gloomier manner, that wanting and not getting leads to unhappiness. But it is oversimplified, as most Buddhists know, there being a bit more required to fully understand the subject.

Economist Robert Heilbroner observed in his influential 1974 book, *Inquiry Into the Human Prospect,* that unlike the divergent views of happiness, there is actually a tremendous consensus on the sources of human misery. In other words, while what people want may differ between individuals, what people don't want includes quite a bit of overlap. Very few people, he observes, enjoy being hungry, impoverished, beaten, robbed, raped, tortured, losing loved ones, etc. I have occasionally—just for fun—asked friends, "Do you enjoy being beaten, robbed, raped, tortured...?" and have found out for myself the truth of Heilbroner's observation. Oddly, most people find the question quite absurd.

To imply, as a vulgar version of Buddhism might, that such unhappiness was due to a person's desire *not* to be raped, beaten, etc., would be expected to get the derision it richly deserved. An educated Buddhist would likely point out that *that* was where the first Noble Truth came in, which is that suffering is unavoidable, but that desires can only make it worse.

But for our purpose, we can say that there are two kinds of unhappiness. I will call them *pain* and *suffering*. Most simply, pain is what you feel when something bad happens to you, and suffering is what your mind does to continue the misery afterwards. I came across this distinction in David Roberts' novel *Shantaram,* as made by his character Abdel Khader Khan. It was Khan's view that although pain could not be avoided, suffering could.

I would tend to agree, but for us to be sure that is true, we need to understand what suffering exactly is. To me, and I think Epictetus would likely agree, suffering is the adding of a personal meaning to pain, which makes it seem more powerful and ominous for the future. (That would certainly be the wrong kind of "handle" to grasp something with.) If you will remember my definition of happiness, you will realize how crucial the imagined future is to our happiness, because that imagined future is in fact its source.

Furthermore, I believe that suffering occurs when we generalize from a painful experience to form a conclusion about either ourselves, life or God. Examples of this are, *I am no good, I am jinxed*, or *Life is unfair* (and yes, *Life is suffering*), or *God doesn't like me* and even *There is no God*. From this you can see how Buddhism could actually produce additional suffering in its quest to relieve suffering, and in fact I believe it does that in this particular case. All three of these generalizations function in the same way to extend our pain— and also our sense of powerlessness—indefinitely into the future.

Why are these three things so significant? It is precisely because they extend into the future. If you remember the premise of this chapter, you will understand why. Happiness is *believing* you will get what you want, not necessarily getting what you want. If you have a negative generalized belief about yourself, life, or God, as cited in the above examples, then you cannot expect to get what you want in the future. If you are no good, jinxed, unlucky or unlovable, you are concluding you will not ever get much of what you want. If life is unfair, you will not get the things you deserve. When you look at the Buddhist phrase, *Life is suffering*, you can see why outsiders say Buddhism is pessimistic—because it forecasts suffering for the future, which is exactly what you don't want.

Aside from being a Buddhist, why would a person do any of that—personalizing or generalizing their pain? It is clearly not rational. Some would say it is simply something we need to stop ourselves from doing, but we know from Wegner's work with ironic processes, our efforts would be likely to fail. The answer is found by understanding the unconscious mind, which we will look at in more detail in Chapter Four, but here's a peek: The best way to cure the tendency, I think you will find, is not to try to suppress it but to understand it, and see through it.

In that vein, I would like to complicate matters even further for a moment. Upon examination it appears that, just as I have explained that there are reflexive thoughts and reflexive emotions, there is also *reflexive suffering* – that is, suffering about suffering. For example, a young person you know dies and you feel grief – that's pain. If you get depressed thinking *life is unfair* – that's suffering. But most of us don't quit there, we eventually get around to thinking *I'm so frustrated, I can't get out of my sorrow... I am so screwed up* – which is reflexive suffering. It should be obvious that in the same way that pain is inevitable, a certain amount of suffering is inevitable as well - as we process our feelings about events and life. But because we are so brainwashed about self-help and happiness we actually increase our unhappiness due to reflexive suffering!

But there is one last issue regarding happiness that we need to take up before leaving the realm of the conscious mind for the murkier worlds of emotion and the unconscious mind, and that is the realm of the imagination.

FANTASIES, WORRIES AND MEMORIES

If you have been reading carefully, you may object to what I am saying that fantasies are what make people happy. That would actually be correct. Another stronger way of saying my premise, *happiness is thinking you are going to get what you want*, is happiness is having a positive fantasy. In fact, fantasies actually make us *more* happy than simply thinking about getting what we want, because in fantasy we are painting the picture of our desire with our imagination and therefore triggering the same endorphins (pleasure hormones) as would be triggered in the actual experience. I recall a time when I endured a one week fast. I made it through that period by repeatedly fantasizing about enjoying an expensive lobster dinner when I concluded the fast. Once I was done fasting, though, I never did eat the lobster dinner, nor did I miss eating it.

Advertisers know how fantasy works and use it to their advantage. One powerful sales technique is called "painting the picture," or more graphically, "selling the sizzle, not the steak," which works by bringing prospective customers into a fantasy. In fact, most ads use this technique. Why do they put a pretty girl next to a car they are trying to sell? Because they are selling the fantasy that a guy who has the car can get the girl. Even the girl can imagine that she's the girl in the ad only made more glamorous. (But for the ad to really work to sell cars to women, there would have to be a hunky guy there instead.) Or the ad might work by selling the ease of loading the car with kids for the soccer moms. Finally, I've noticed how SUV ads promote the vehicles by portraying them driving through mountains and sunsets. Few people ever use the four-wheel drive on their SUVs, but that doesn't stop the fantasy of such rugged and picturesque driving from being a popular allure.

But fantasies as happiness motivators do have a couple of drawbacks. A fantasy can be unfulfilled, and the moment it gets punctured, unhappiness will creep in. Likewise, if the fantasy *is* fulfilled, it may soon start to wear off. You drive the new car home and put it in the garage. You marry Prince Charming and move into the castle. Then what do you do? Obviously, there are two options: get depressed, or start a new fantasy. You might plan an adventure trip with the new car. Convince Prince Charming to have kids. Or fantasize about having an affair with the neighboring knight. And the game continues.

Some people try to stay focused on work, which keeps them occupied and not thinking too much about these things. It also helps them to fantasize about all the things they can soon buy or the increased prestige that success at work may bring. And the game continues.

Perhaps they might then fantasize accumulating wealth and power. But there is no evidence that even wealth and power produce happiness. They can fantasize about buying another yacht or another company, or if rising to political power, even about conquering another country. And the game would continue. Or they could fantasize about leaving it all behind. But the game would still continue.

Others may try to help other people, which is rewarding as they see the benefits others receive and the gratitude they get back.

But subtly they start thinking about how those benefits will multiply, or how to multiply the benefits themselves. And the game continues.

Still others may try to better themselves by learning to paint or play an instrument or take a class. And they begin to imagine themselves playing before audiences or applying their knowledge. And the game continues.

Next people might start to think there is something wrong with them, and go to a therapist. That might help them feel better by getting things off of their chests. But they would soon start imagining how much better they will feel once they are emotionally healed. And the game would continue.

Finally, people might start to see through the game and start to more deeply question the meaning of life. Perhaps they would become spiritual or religious and seek answers there. They take a workshop or go to church, and then begin to fantasize about a more spiritual or holy way of living, about the happiness of enlightenment or heaven, and that makes them happy. Still, the game continues.

My point is, fantasy, even with its downside, is pretty much inevitable. It is built into the human brain, no doubt as a survival mechanism. Being able to use our imagination helps us to mock up possible scenarios in order to make decisions, and that is precisely what has helped humans accomplish great deeds and fulfill visions. Psychologically, it also serves us as an outlet, much like dreams. Fantasies can compensate for unfulfilling realities by, in essence, getting an advance on the paycheck of the future. But unlike a Payday Loan, the costs are quite low if done moderately and with good sense. As long as you limit the amount of time daydreaming and don't require all your fantasies to become realities, you are likely to be fine.

However, if you lie on the couch fantasizing about being rich instead of looking for a job, or if you try to actualize the fantasy of sleeping with your neighbor's wife (or husband), the consequences could be negative. Furthermore, if one becomes attached to the idea of the fantasy becoming reality, the disillusionment could be quite painful. This is why it seems so catastrophic when you get dumped by your dream girl or dream guy. Not only is there the objective loss of someone who is starting to be important, but also the death of a dream and an imagined future together. Sometimes the grieving for that future and that dream is more intense than the loss of the companionship itself, especially when the relationship has been short and its imagined version still strong.

Loss of the fantasy, rather than the actuality, is precisely what the Buddhists mean when they say that desires cause suffering. In fact, it is not the desire itself that causes the suffering, because every day most people are forced to forego a number of desires, just for practical purposes. The desire to lay a little longer in bed, the desire for an extra cup of coffee or a donut, all may be put aside for reasons of time, calories, or other practical reasons without much suffering. But to lose the chance for a great vacation at the last minute, because your work schedule has changed, or the chance at a million dollar investment, can cause quite a bit of suffering—even though, you could argue, that you are no worse off, since the only thing you've lost is something you hadn't even obtained yet. So in fact, it is not the desire but the fantasy that causes the impact, whether the impact is pleasurable or painful.

The other side of fantasy is *worry*. Worry is essentially the opposite of happiness: Worry that you will not get the things you want, lose the things you have, or get things you don't want, like an abusive boss or spouse, noisy neighbors or a bout of ill health. These thoughts produce immediate stress reactions in the body, just as those actual events would.

On the upside, it is quite clear that worry is also necessary for human survival, perhaps even more so than fantasy. If a person doesn't worry about some future event (think about or imagine negative consequences or possible harmful events), they may not take adequate precautions. Of course, excessive and chronic worry can create stress and other problems, but the natural tendency to worry sometimes is probably healthy to a large degree. You might raise an objection here, asking *Doesn't worry cause stress, and isn't that a bad thing?* I don't disagree but am only saying worry is natural, even unavoidable to a certain degree, and actually useful in moderation.

Despite the popularity of the song "Don't Worry, Be Happy" in the 1980s, and the bestseller *Don't Sweat the Small Stuff - And It's All Small Stuff* by Richard Carlson in the 1990s, worry and sweating the small stuff is still going on, now with the *added* worry, that we are worrying too much. When friends ask me for advice about how much they are worrying, I always tell them, "Don't worry about *it* (the worrying, that is)! Just write it down." The reason this works is that worries are nature's warning system and writing them down reduces the repetitive nature of worrying by reassuring the mind that its concerns are being taking seriously. This can help shortcut chronic worrying. If you find yourself without a pen, the technique I offer in Chapter 7 works as well.

People who don't worry are like people who have no fear. They blaze across the sky like a meteor but soon burn out. Or, as they say in the world of espionage, *There are old agents, and there are bold agents, but there are no old AND bold agents.* I'll go more into this in the next chapter about emotions, but the essence of the issue is that *a little* worry, even though it produces some unhappiness, is beneficial, because it is designed to protect us from what we *really* don't want. Interestingly, in fact, a 2013 study by Dr Freider Lang in Germany concluded that pessimism about the future (worry) encouraged people to live more carefully and actually prolonged their lives.

Is it possible to worry too much? Yes, excess worry can cause stress and impede performance. But like much else, the problem isn't in the item, but rather in the use or abuse.

Even if you aren't convinced about the positive side of fantasy and worry in maintaining well-being, there is always memory to consider. Unlike what is preached by Eckhart Tolle in his bestselling *The Power of Now*, we can't simply become happy by cutting off our worries of the future through mental discipline and practice, because of one thing—the *past*.

The past influences our happiness through two processes: memory and the unconscious. While it is probably possible to push away memories, or more likely distract yourself from them, you can't avoid their influence as a subconscious pressure on your psyche that could possibly surface at an unforeseeable time. Furthermore, I suggest that despite the popularity of Tolle's book, pushing away memories is not an effort that is likely to succeed, and it can possibly create an unhealthy backlash, as I will also describe in Chapter Four on the unconscious.

To be fair, Tolle's insight that we can at any time experience the Now is a powerful one. Imagine you are walking down a street. It doesn't matter whether you are rich or poor, whether you had a fight with your spouse or just made love, the experience of walking down the street would be the same. It would also be the same if you were experiencing it alone, in and of itself, or with another. Being so fully into that experience of walking down the street, as if for the first time, offers you an avenue of escape from any worries and memories that may be plaguing you.

A break in the pattern of obsessive thoughts can certainly be useful. If we could train ourselves to do this *all the time*, Tolle argues, we would be happy and content. A cynic would argue that we would also be depriving ourselves of the pleasure of our memories, and I think Tolle would concede that point. But he would say being *in the Now* is worth it and that the experience of the current moment could be just as pleasurable as any memory or even more.

One could also argue that being present to the "now" of being at the dentist's office would be less pleasurable, but I think Tolle *would* argue that point, saying that it is our fears and memories which actually make the experience worse, not being "in the now."

But my criticism is different. In fact, I have a couple. I'd say that Tolle is making precisely the same mistake as we do normally in our ordinary thinking, which is trying to hold on to an experience—only this time it is an inner experience rather than an outer one. While some people might have a major Zen experience of being "in the now," most will not, and those rest of us will be trying to change ourselves and accomplish this through thought suppression, much in the exact same way as positive thinkers. Even those who do have that rare Zen experience may end up being caught in the trap of trying to recreate it over and over, wracking up failure after failure, and dooming themselves eventually to disillusionment and self-deprecation.

I also suspect that trying to always stay "in the Now" prevents a person from thinking things through and therefore developing depth and wisdom. In the Now, the only mistake you can make is *not* "being in the now" and the only lesson you can learn is how to "be" there, creating a rather shallow environment for real growth.

Finally, to me, memories, worries and fantasies are products not just causes. Excessive worrying, fantasizing and ruminating about the past are symptoms, not the problem. The very fact that nearly all people engage in all three but differ in both the content and the amount, signifies to me that the content and amount, not the activity itself, are what is most important for that individual. And that content is often stored in the unconscious mind. Trying to stay in the now is ignoring that content.

Fans of Eckhart Tolle will say that he does indeed acknowledge the content of the unconscious mind in his description of the *pain body*, his term for the physio-emotional recording of our past traumas that lives inside us. But my argument is that Tolle sees this pain body as pretty much an enemy or a obstacle to avoid, in order to stay in the Now. That approach, in my opinion, is misguided, a little risky, and likely to fail as I will attempt to show in the next two chapters on emotions and the unconscious mind.

The short version of my argument is that unexpressed emotions in their stored state are quite powerful and only ignored at one's own risk, because they can fester and therefore cause sabotage. In any case, the healthier resurfacing of an old emotion, although it can be quite painful, passes quickly and has little to do with our overall happiness in the long term.

REASONS FOR HAPPINESS?

As I was finishing this chapter, I came across yet another happiness book. This one was called *Happy for No Reason* by Marcy Shimoff. I laughed to myself when I saw the title, because that title makes a statement that is the opposite of what I am trying to explain. By an odd coincidence, I was talking about it to a friend who is a book editor, and she mentioned she had worked on that book. I noted my objection to the title, and she responded that the book was actually quite successful. I was intrigued, so I looked it up on Amazon.com and found that it contained some 21 tips gained from interviewing one hundred happy people. The *Editors Weekly Review* on the site called the book "sound and commonsensical ..." Some of the tips mentioned are to practice forgiveness, make peace with yourself, or write a letter to a higher power.

Still fascinated, I visited a bookstore and purchased a copy. As it turned out it was well-written book, similar to many in the New Age self-help genre, but more practical than most. Essentially Shimoff advises people to "go within" to find a wellspring of happiness, which is a topic I will explore in Chapter Five. What struck me was the fact that this particular book was so popular. Apparently, a lot of people would like to be happy for no reason. That could be because they have some reasons to be unhappy, and want to get rid of those reasons. I personally would prefer to be happy for a good reason, but I suspect that most people like the idea of being happy all the time and thus not subject to the vagaries of life.

Of course, there is an easy way to accomplish being happy all the time, one even more popular than the book. That is to take happy pills, also known as anti-depressant medication, like Prozac, handed out by doctors quite liberally these days. Of course, getting a doctor's prescription is more expensive than buying the book and has the added stigma of "taking medication."

Now, I am not suggesting that Ms. Shimoff is prescribing the literary equivalent of a happy pill, in fact I liked her book far better than Eckhart Tolle's and can actually recommend it, because it has a number of practical methods people can easily apply. Maybe the book would be better named *Happiness for a Good Inner Reason*, but probably it wouldn't have sold as well. In fact, my only criticism is that like most of its genre there simply are times when that approach will not work – which is what my book is for. . What I am saying is that the *appeal* of the book (not its content) to its self-help audience is in a way nothing more than an attempt to avoid unhappiness. In any case, if we imagine actually being happy for no reason, it really doesn't look too much different than being on happy pills, with some of the same potential drawbacks. As we have often heard, *pain is nature's way of telling you something's wrong*, so pain and suffering may well be signals to draw your attention to a circumstance to try to rectify it. And there may be times when rectifying it may be more difficult than it simply trying to come to peace with yourself, or more complex than writing a letter to a higher power.

But let's go back to the notion of actual "happy pills." Unfortunately for the modern psychiatrist, dealing with unhappiness is more complex than merely prescribing the proper dose of an anti-depressant. In 2010, a *New York Times* series of articles presented a retrospective on psychotherapy that showed a new direction. In two of these articles, one entitled "Depression's Upside," and the other "Mind over Meds," the authors noted that some leading researchers and therapists were starting to question the dominant model of medicating people and replacing it with a problem-solving focus. Medicated people may feel better, but they end up being less motivated to solve the real problems that are often causing their depression, such as problems in their relationships, work and families. Instead of medicating them, coaching for resolving their issues not only made them feel better but produced longer lasting results.

I will note that, consistent with my own theory, these problems are typically experienced when people are thinking they're not getting what they really want in those areas, as well as getting what they *don't* want. The flip side of Epictetus' dictum is knowing what you *can* change and taking the right steps to do it.

Having eliminated simple fixes, we now need to leave the world of the mind and travel downward into the emotions and the unconscious. Considering that since pain and suffering are emotional states, the first step towards more fully understanding happiness is to understand more about the emotions and how they work, and the different flavors of unhappiness they may produce, and with that knowledge perhaps find a solution to the question of happiness.

CHAPTER 3

MOTION OF EMOTIONS

There is an old joke that goes like this:
Q: What is the epitome of mixed emotions?
A: Watching your mother-in-law go off a cliff in your new Mercedes.

It's a corny old joke, probably sexist and in bad taste, but it does make the point that your emotions are linked to getting what you want or don't want.

Strangely though, it seems that only in the last few decades people and social scientists have noticed the emotions as something worth understanding as opposed to simply controlling or repressing. The world's religions have little to say on the matter, other than that human emotions cause problems. Here are a few quotes and their sources:

The Bible: *He that is slow to anger is better than the mighty.* [Proverbs 16:32]

The Buddha: *He who loves 50 people has 50 woes; he who loves no one has no woes.* {attributed to Buddha }

The Qur'an: *Be not grieving, and you shall have the upper hand if you are believers.* [Al-e-Imran, 3:139]

The statements are not wrong, it's just that few of us ever reach such supposedly desirable states of emotional high ground.

Of course, all of it was written before the development of modern psychology, so any understanding of the interior of the human mind was still obscure. And I suppose, if there is no understanding of them, then controlling the emotions is the only option.

However, even with the development of psychology, our understanding of emotions was slow to develop. Freud wrote little about it, preferring—in accordance with the times—to devote any explanation instead to instincts or drives. Likewise, Carl Jung spent little time on emotions, preferring to analyze cultural archetypes rather than human feelings. Possibly, the oversight was due to those vast intellects not being as in touch with their feelings as they were with their particular genius. Fritz Perls was probably the first person to start the process of working with human emotions as we know them, developing his Gestalt therapy in the 1960s and in the work it later inspired at such places as the Esalen Institute in California. That wave seems to have spread out beyond the human potential movement and then back into psychology. In the 1990s, Daniel Goleman's *Emotional Intelligence* became a best seller, bringing our purview of emotions fully into the mainstream.

But we need to understand emotions better in our inquiry into happiness, because there are differing explanations about what suffering, unhappiness and depression are all about. Some of the main theories are that unhappiness and depression are both forms of sadness, or conflict from unexpressed emotions lying just below the surface, or anger turned inwards. And then there is *my* theory, that unhappiness is more simple: thinking that we are not getting what we want. Let's take a look at the terrain.

WHAT ARE EMOTIONS?

So what exactly are emotions? The word *emotion* is based on root words from Latin meaning "to move out." They are feelings that occur in the body that may be triggered by events or by thoughts. Emotions are truly different than thoughts, even though some religious practitioners and therapists tend to blend the two, saying emotions are simply by-products of thoughts. It is true that most emotions have a mental component, but the existence of emotions in babies and animals proves their precedence over thoughts. We also all notice that while thoughts appear to be located in the head, feelings are seated in the torso of the body, which would seem to indicate the probability of a separate origin. We are starting to see that chemical and hormonal reactions in the gut seem to be integral to the feelings that emotions produce.

Why do emotions exist? The most probable reason is survival. A fight or flight response is aided by the hormonal arousal of fear and anger Feelings of love aid bonding and allow family, friendship and community to arise, all things needed for human survival. It is my contention that each and every emotion is important and valid, even though emotions can be mistakenly stimulated in many situations, such as anger due to a misunderstanding.

In Goleman's *Emotional Intelligence,* an anecdote is told about a man who through an operation for brain disease lost all of his emotional processing abilities and was content no matter what happened to him. In short, he became the ideal of all religions—a man not just slow to anger, but impossible to anger. Or be afraid. Or make jealous. His inability to feel led him to value everything equally. Unfortunately, his equanimity led to poor judgment, because nothing was more important to him than anything else. He soon lost his marriage, and eventually lost his job and became homeless. He was unfazed by any of it, but his case shows that emotions are important at the very least for prioritizing values.

TYPES OF EMOTIONS

Psychologists sometimes list four main emotional clusters: Love, grief (or sadness), fear, and anger. These are the simple emotions. There are also complex emotions, which are emotions based on social factors, including guilt, shame, envy, and jealousy. As sociologist Thomas Scheff at the University of California, Santa Barbara, has pointed out, there are also "lite" versions of emotion, like frustration instead of anger, anxiety instead of fear, and embarrassment instead of shame.

I would like to explore each of these emotions, both simple and complex, and show how they relate to each other, and why they are functional to society and important to the individual. I will also explore how controlling, working out, and/or releasing emotions can be helpful in reducing unhappiness and resolving personal issues.

Interestingly, love and grief seem to be linked emotions. They are both bonding emotions, one occurring in response to successful linking and the other when bonding is unsuccessful. You may love someone, but if you lose them, you feel grief. Sadness is another way of describing the feeling of loss when it is a little less intense. As I have said, love is essential for the formation of human family and community. Likewise, the "lite" version of love is friendship or liking.

Is grief functional? At times it would seem not, especially when it can be so paralyzing, but the important thing to remember is that the alternative would be worse. If grief and loss were not so devastating, fewer attempts to repair family and friendship would be the inevitable result. So in the big picture, grief is highly functional for human society, even though it may be debilitating for an individual. Since human survival is dependent on the formation of human social groups for the species to survive, many social functions must be deeply physically or culturally ingrained.

Incest taboos are another example of this phenomenon of something that is individually felt but socially necessary. Anthropologists believe that since genetic issues can only develop over a number of generations, the real reason for incest taboos and the disgust that violations of it engender is not the protection of genes, as we might expect, but the protection of social roles. It is hard for people to envision the same feelings for parents as for lovers, which is all for the best, in keeping family roles and duties clear.

Fear and anger also seem to be linked. They are aversive emotions that arise when people think they're about to get something they don't want (i.e., something harmful) or *not* get something they do want. A person can be afraid of being robbed, or afraid they will not get the promotion they need. Anger seems to be triggered by a split second calculation (even though unconscious) about one's relative power in a situation, for example, that to stand and fight may work better than to flee. A parent who is worried to death about a child's late arrival home and then gets angry when the child finally arrives provides a good example of an unconscious reaction to the change of one's power in a situation.

BOREDOM AND DEPRESSION

Boredom is an interesting emotion, and one that I rarely see discussed, despite its frequency and its importance in human motivation. Why do people take books to the beach? Why do they watch so much television? Why do people have affairs? Why do people drink and take drugs or do risky activities, everything from riding motorcycles to skydiving, to becoming soldiers of fortune? Why do kings and dictators who have everything invade other countries? The answer is probably boredom. But this last example is illustrative.

It is likely that fantasy plays an important role in preventing boredom, as I have discussed in the previous chapter. We are happiest when we have something to fantasize about, specifically getting something we want. But what if we already have everything we want? Then the only option is distraction. That's why we normal folks watch television or take books to the beach. But a king or dictator has much more elaborate entertainments, such as jugglers, jesters, dancing girls, hunting parties, even jousts or gladiators from what I have seen in the movies. But sooner or later those things get old. Eventually the ruler thinks, *I would be much happier if I could just get rid of my enemies in Country X*. He gets to work at raising an army and suddenly feels better as he starts to fantasize about his victory. Of course, once he wins the war, the whole thing starts over again, and suddenly he feels depressed.

Boredom in general is a reaction to a perceived lack of stimulation. It seems possible that there is an evolutionary reason for boredom which may be to keep humans active and moving around. This seems very functional from a survival perspective. If you look at animals, they seems to have numerous scanning activities built in. Predators alone benefit from sheer concentration. Prey benefit from sensitivity to their environment which likely translates into a need for stimulation. Of course, we humans are both predators *and* prey, so we often have conflicting needs.

And what about depression? Is that an emotion? If we look at depression and feel it out, the closest emotion is sadness of some form, which is in the grief cluster. However, psychologists tell us that depression is anger turned inwards. Is that true?

It is my belief that both are partially true but the statements obscure a larger truth about the nature of depression. There is sadness in depression, that is clear. But sadness at what? The sadness, it would seem for most people, is from repeatedly not being able to get what one wants. Or, of course, repeatedly getting what one *doesn't* want. Since, in the last chapter, we defined suffering as a state of pain enhanced by a belief about life, self, or God that extends into the future, then this fits in totally.

But does anger explain anything? Anger is closely related to frustration—anger "lite"— and we can see that if a person repeatedly doesn't get what they want, or repeatedly gets what they don't want, that person could get frustrated. It is likely, therefore, that both sadness and anger are not causes of depression, but expressions of it at different times, or in different people. That is not to say therapists shouldn't encourage depressed people to express their anger, because such expression will reduce their emotional burden. But it does mean that a long term solution is unlikely to occur until the depressed person can either change or accept their circumstances.

Of course, here we have to feel sorry for our poor kings who despite having everything they could possibly want, cannot get out of the same happiness trap as the less fortunate masses. I once heard a phrase from Buddhism or Hinduism that went something like this: *Desire once satisfied, craves more desire.* Like I said before, the game continues...

CONTROLLING OUR EMOTIONS

Can emotions be controlled? People tend to disagree about this, but certainly the expression of emotions can. Gordon Clanton, in his 1987 book *Jealousy* gives the example of a couple arguing in car that has been pulled over by the police. Can the people stop the argument? Most people can, he reports, even though some will be resuming their argument after the officer leaves.

But what happens to the emotion if it is not expressed at all? Here psychologists differ. There is evidence that the expression of an emotion stimulates a further reaction, as adrenaline is released, and the body's physiology is aroused. This line of thinking leads some psychologists, particularly practitioners of the new "positive psychology," to believe that negative emotional expression should be inhibited as much as possible to avoid further reaction.

However, psychologists who subscribe to classical theory would debate this as would many others. You cannot inhibit an emotion, they would say, only its expression. Inhibiting its expression causes stress to be stored in the body and a charged memory in the subconscious. Freud's early training was in the treatment of female hysteria, a Victorian era mental illness that seems to have nearly completely disappeared with the lowering of inhibitions since that era.

Anger seems to provide the best case for inhibiting emotional expression. When you get angry and express it, that expression triggers a fear response in your target and possibly even in bystanders. Then they get stimulated and respond with anger or fear. Their response to your anger may re-stimulate you to get even angrier if you feel threatened or even if you feel unheard. But there is an alternative to either inhibition or unrestrained expression, and that is to express it, but use a cushion to lighten the blow. Saying "I'm angry but I don't want to feel angry," or something similar before or even after the angry reaction takes people off the spot, and prevents an anger spiral from occurring.

Interestingly, there are some people who seem to love being angry, and society has developed a term for them–*rage-aholics.* These people typically refuse to control their anger, and it is worth a minute exploring why. You'll recall that I said that anger and fear are related emotions but differ in terms of an assessment of power. An angry person feels powerful, especially if his or her emotion scares other people. It's not hard to see how that feeling could become addictive if it helps them get what they want. It also probably helps them resist their innermost feelings of powerlessness, much in the same way that smaller dogs are often the biggest barkers. Finally, I suspect that the rage-aholic often feels somewhat purged and cleansed after an emotional tantrum, which is why I like to joke that anger is really depression turned *outwards* – the converse of the popular idea that depression is anger turned inwards. Anger replaces an inner feeling of disempowerment with one of outer power.

As I was revising this chapter, I came across an article based on research from Richard Stephens of Keele University in England. His study demonstrated that swearing allowed people to withstand physical pain for longer periods of time. Armed with this knowledge, I happily applied it the next time I was in a bad mood by swearing loudly while in my car, and I can report that it works quite well—even better since I know I don't have to feel guilty about being negative!

EMOTIONS: CAUSES OR EFFECTS?

The standard explanation of emotions is that they are triggered by a stimulus. But why is anything in particular a stimulus? Some things are obvious - a sudden noise or jolt could trigger fear as a possible sign of danger. But other things are more complex. When you hear a song the first time, you are reacting to the sound and words. But when you hear a song again and again, you may react to the memories of the sensations you experienced while listening to the song on earlier occasions. That's what is happening when, as the saying goes, "they're playing 'our' song."

Psychology adds to the discussion by pointing out that the external stimulus is often less important than an interior one, such as a thought or memory. But the interior stimulus may also trigger emotions that are hard to understand, because memories are not always *consciously* associated with every experience that is emotionally triggered. In other words, a person may have a reaction to an external event or stimulus that does not consciously remind them of a specific memory, but it still triggers an emotional response. Quite often, if the person tries to examine the source of the trigger, they are reminded of a memory that explains the reaction, but that memory was not in mind when it was triggered. It is possible that the memory flashed by so quickly that it barely registered before it created the reaction which then overshadowed it. We have our first inkling of unconscious or semi-conscious thought right there. In any case, it puts us on notice that the link between thought and feeling is more complex than we might have believed.

Emotions can also trigger thoughts, or so it seems. You may have heard the line in the song, "When you're smiling, the whole world smiles with you." It refers in part, not just to the fact that people return smiles given to them, but also I think, to the fact that when you are in a good mood, everything that comes to you is interpreted in a different way than when you are in a bad mood.

Are thoughts causing emotions or are they effects of emotions? This may seem like a chicken or egg argument, but it is important and interesting to see how perspectives differ on this. Psychology tends to see thoughts as effects, determined by earlier emotions that have been stored in the unconscious mind. However, most religions tend to see thoughts as causes. I remember a Michael Moore speaking routine in his 1997 movie, *The Big One*, in which he reminisced that in his Catholic school the nuns taught that a thought that simply passed through the mind was a *venial* sin, but a mortal sin was one that a person entertained for more than five seconds. In any case, we can think of many examples from every religion advising us not to think thoughts that are doubtful, envious, judgmental, and so on. Self-help tends to also focus on thoughts as causes, telling us to think positively in order to bring a more positive outcome to our lives.

Similarly, in Buddhism, the statement from the Four Noble Truths is that desires, or at least attachments, cause suffering. This is true on its face, but it begs another question, which is: What's the cause of the attachment? Buddhism would state that the cause of attachment could have been due to something in a previous lifetime. But that is skipping some important steps.

From the perspective of psychology, we could even say the opposite – that suffering is often the cause of attachment. Looking at addictions, the most severe of attachments, most people would agree that something must have already been wrong for a person to fall victim to an addiction. With drugs, alcohol, sexual, or gambling addictions, we have the understanding that there's an underlying cause, possibly from childhood, for which the addiction is a symptom. Interestingly, sex addiction happens most frequently with people who have strict sexual upbringings, just as alcoholism is more prevalent in children of families that don't drink socially.

I once talked with a friend who was studying under a spiritual teacher in the Advaita (non-dualistic) tradition of Hinduism. I asked him what the fellow was teaching. He responded that one of the things his teacher had said was: "Control causes fear." I have to admit that my jaw dropped when I heard this, because it is the reverse of what nearly all psychologists say, which is that control, as in controlling behavior, is generally *motivated* by fear. Unfortunately, my scoffing ended the conversation, but it would have been interesting to find out how my friend explained it, though I have to doubt it would have been convincing. In any case, this incident well illustrates the predisposition of the spiritual and religious viewpoint to see thoughts as causing emotions, and not the other way around.

Actually, the scientific research has largely proven the opposite of the spiritual view. A number of studies have shown that thoughts are almost like echoes, repeating after another part of us has already decided or reacts to something. For example, you say to yourself, *I am going to go to the refrigerator*, after you have *already* put that behavior into motion. Another example is you get angry first and then you think, "that pisses me off!" The thought follows like an echo of the original impulse. So much so, in fact, that Wegner titled a later book he wrote *The Illusion of Conscious Will*, making the point that our conscious thoughts aren't always a conscious choice.

So if psychology is correct, and thoughts are to a large degree symptomatic rather than causative, then attempts to correct our thoughts would again be superficial and likely fail, as I have argued before for completely different reasons.

I mentioned earlier how stimuli can be triggered by unconscious or semi-conscious factors, as well as by memories. This opens up a can of worms, if you think about it, taking into account that our thoughts are affected by enormous numbers of variables, both within and without.

It is most likely that both views of causation are partially true. Thoughts produce feelings and other times feelings produce thoughts. The question would be better asked: *Where in the cycle of thought and emotion is intervention most likely to succeed?* The answer is a key point, and I think it may be in our thoughts and feelings *about* our feelings, not those thoughts and feelings themselves. Again, the perception is what is important, not the reality. It's how we think about or perceive things, not the things themselves, that makes the difference in how we experience life, (or in other words, what I call *reflexive* emotions.)

LAYERS OF EMOTION

It is an old truism that we humans are self-conscious. That is to say, we are conscious of ourselves, and we are even conscious of our consciousness. That capacity has also been called *reflexive thinking*, and occasionally *meta-thought*. Much of philosophy and psychology, as well as bits of the various social sciences, are devoted to understanding thought and so fit into that category.

However, less well explored is our reflexivity when it comes to emotions. Not only do we have thoughts about our thoughts, but we have thoughts and feelings about our emotions, as I mentioned in the Prologue. It is rare for an adult to have a simple emotion. They are typically layered, one over another. Emotions like jealousy or anger are often covering other emotions like fear. Shame is an emotion that we often have about having other emotions. When a person denies that they are jealous, they are demonstrating three levels of emotion: shame covering jealousy covering fear. If you probe them, a fourth emotion may arise, anger.

Growing up, a child is constantly learning the contexts in which certain emotions are not acceptable. Those contexts may be fairly arbitrary, set according to parental and social values, but those contexts don't stop the child from having the unacceptable emotions. The child still has them, and so a level of guilt, shame, or repression about those emotions gets created, a kind of the layering effect. This fact has enormous consequences in psychology and in the argument I <u>am</u> making in this book.

And here we have yet another argument against conventional positive thinking used in self-help. Not wanting to have "negative feelings" doesn't make those feelings go away. Rather, it creates even more of what you don't want, another layer of guilt or shame about your feelings.

I often hear people say things like, "I'm trying to be positive, but I can't help feeling (something negative)," which means there are now two emotions, the original one plus guilt, in this case. Or, "I don't want anyone to see me when I am being so negative," adding shame now on top of the original.

What I will show later in this book is that, unlike the simplistic solutions offered by self-help books and gurus, there are actual interventions you can make into your thinking and feeling process to change the trajectory of your thoughts and feelings without invalidating them. But in order to do that, we need to continue exploring the workings of our psychological nature and see how we are not doing anything "wrong." In that pursuit, we now look into the "distance" from which we think about our feelings, because that seems to have an effect as well.

BOUNDARIES AND EMOTIONAL DISTANCE

Some people you may know are constantly at the mercy of their emotions, and others at the opposite extreme are like calculators, predictably non-emotional. In general, there is a somewhat accurate stereotype that men are more emotionally distant than women. What accounts for this distance, and is there an ideal distance for the purposes of living and relating?

Ernest Hartmann addresses this question in his book, *Boundaries in the Mind.* Hartmann notes a number of characteristics of individuals with what he calls *thick* and *thin boundaries*, in reference to their behavior and way of relating to others. For instance, people with thick boundaries tend to be quite organized and keep everything in its designated place, while people with thin boundaries appear to be somewhat disorganized and operate spontaneously rather than according to a planned schedule. The differences are even more pronounced.

People with very thin boundaries may have difficulty distinguishing dreams from memories (*Did that really happen, or did I just dream it happened?*). They are also more likely to spend time daydreaming and to suffer from nightmares. Thin-boundaried people tend to fall in love more easily, they may have more identity issues, and they may even experience themselves as both child and adult, or male and female, all at the same time. They are more prone to unusual perceptual experiences, such as *déjà vu*, and feelings of clairvoyance or premonition. Hartmann found that both psychotics and artists tend to have thin boundaries.

In contrast, people with thick interpersonal boundaries often end up in fields like sales or athletics, or math or the military, where their ability to push aside their feelings (be "thick skinned") is a virtue. But the downside is that they tend to become alienated and out of touch with their own intuitions and feelings, as well as out of touch with other individuals.

While people's boundaries tend to be somewhat stable, it is also true that we have varying distances, or boundaries, from different emotions as well. Some people have strong boundaries against specific emotions that don't fit in with their upbringing or social setting. For example, some people are taught that anger is not appropriate. Others may feel like jealousy is a harmful emotion. It is a truism that emotions do not always go away, they are typically just repressed. Repression, of course, is that process by which unacceptable emotions are pushed down into the unconscious mind, where they continue to lurk in the darkness, if you will, ready to spring back when one's boundaries are weakened.

On the other hand, being too close to your emotions may also be unhealthy. Incarceration or institutionalization is a possible outcome for those who are completely unable to manage their emotions. For most people, being at the whim of moods is a common result of not having much distance from their emotions.

Interestingly, in my experience, moods are simply the effect of unexpressed emotions existing just below consciousness. They are typically the result of unprocessed emotional reactions to events that have occurred. Freud called these recent and unprocessed reactions *daily residue*, and found they made up much of the more superficial content of dreams. Beneath that superficial level is what he referred to as "psychologically significant material," which he saw as a link between mundane, everyday events and the deeper layer of repressed trauma.

For example, a car may honk at you, and you might not experience any emotional reaction to it. Or you might experience a reaction but not acknowledge it, adding it to your daily residue of minor issues. But if the driver called you a name that you were sensitive to due to a past traumatic event, it might cause a deeper, more significant reaction, even though you might try to shrug it off.

Moods might also arise from emotions that are brought back up by dreams. That, I think, accounts for most of the "waking up on the wrong side of bed" phenomenon that many people experience.

In any case, a mood is typically due to an emotion that is too close to be repressed and just a little too far down to be consciously processed. By adjusting your distance, you can bring the emotion closer in range where you can deal with it. Of course, you can also do the opposite, repress it even further out of range, so it goes a way for a while longer.

The process of bringing an emotion closer is at the core of all successful psychotherapy, in my opinion. The sociologist Thomas Scheff calls this ideal position *participant/observer* to describe when a person is half in the experience and half outside of it, just enough to be objective. I saw a good example of this when coming across a TV report about the aftermath of Hurricane Katrina in 2005. A woman was describing how the crisis hotline where she worked was overwhelmed with calls from displaced victims for weeks after the crisis had ended. She was asked, "Why couldn't the victims have just talked with each other to reduce their stressful emotions?" Her answer was that since they were all victims, no one was outside the crisis enough emotionally to be able to hear the others with any distance. In other words, talking with another person who was also too under-distanced from the crises only re-stimulated the traumatic feeling, rather than start to heal it. That could only happen when at least one person had enough emotional distance from the crisis.

Some precision about this has been developed by the Re-Evaluation Counseling movement, or as it is popularly known, "co-counseling." Started in the 1950s by Harvey Jackins, co-counseling has existed outside the therapeutic profession but has influenced many therapists and psychologists, and seems to have influenced Thomas Scheff as well.

The basic theory is similar to humanistic psychology in that it sees people as essentially and naturally good and happy, but injured by traumas in early life that created wounds and negative beliefs. Through attention and empathy, individuals are taught to counsel each other to help heal and readjust their beliefs. By adjusting the emotional distance through dialogue, role-playing, and repeating a specific type of affirmation called a "contradiction" (in that it contradicts a negative belief), the recipient of the counseling is brought to the ideal point of Scheff's participant/observer position, and a powerful emotional discharge can occur. The negative emotion naturally and cleanly "moves out"... and is gone!

The first time I saw this demonstrated, it seemed miraculous, so precise was the methodology in getting to the emotion. I immediately signed up to learn the method and have found it to be immensely useful.

Unfortunately, during the training, I found out there was a little thing they called *chronic distress patterns*. These, as one might suspect, are chronic issues that, even though the related emotion gets discharged, seem to persist. The view was that chronic patterns, though pesky, were eventually healable through continued work. However, what I noticed was that the trainers, most of whom had been practicing co-counseling for a decade or more, still had chronic issues that seemed to be very deeply anchored. I am not devaluing the process—emotional discharge is powerfully cleansing and healing—but it did not seem to go deep enough to reach the heart of the matter, despite being one of the deepest emotional release processes I've experienced.

If emotions and pent-up emotions were indeed the only impediment, then success in life would be just a little more difficult than Epictetus depicted, but not a lot. However, it turns out, the emotions are just the tip of the iceberg, and as you know, most of the iceberg is under water. Even if our emotions can be released, it would be a little like trying to melt the iceberg with a big magnifying glass. True, that's faster than not trying at all or just letting the sun do it, but the biggest part, those pesky chronic issues and their deeper emotions, take some real excavation.

In the next chapter, the exploration of our psychological nature takes us deeper into the realm of our unconscious mind, a realm that Epictetus didn't have to consider but we modern humans do, in learning how to live successfully.

CHAPTER 4

THE UNCONSCIOUS MIND

A professor of mine used to remark that the unconscious mind is a lot like God. No one has seen Him, but everyone has seen his Works. In other words, like God for a believer, the unconscious has left clues as to its existence. But before we begin look for those clues, there is a distinction to be made.

Essentially, for purposes of our discussion, there are two kinds of unconscious mind. The first is the *unnoticed* unconscious, or what I'll call the "subconscious mind;" and the second is the *deep* (unnoticeable) unconscious, from now on referred to as the "unconscious mind." Much of what we have been discussing in the past chapters is the subconscious mind, in which thoughts and feelings go by without our paying much attention to them.

While most of us go through the day unaware of what is causing fluctuations in our moods, developing a habit of paying attention to subtle feelings going on can bring much insight. In fact, a major argument of this book is that a key to reducing unhappiness and promoting emotional harmony is in correctly addressing our subconscious mind in which are often those unnoticed feelings. But it is also crucial to understand the role of the deep unconscious to understand why my theory works the way it does and why happiness cannot consistently be produced by acts of mental control.

THE DISCOVERY OF THE UNCONSCIOUS

So much do the ideas of modern psychology permeate our world view that it is difficult to imagine the importance of those ideas in changing our culture over the last hundred or so years. Take a look at these passages from the Bible for contrast between now and the earlier paradigm:

The wise shall inherit glory: but shame shall be the promotion of fools. [Proverbs 3:34-35]

Understand, ye brutish among the people: and ye fools, when will ye be wise? [Psalms 94:7-9]

One of Crete's own prophets has said it: "Cretans are always liars, evil brutes, lazy gluttons." [Titus 1:12]

For the congregation of hypocrites shall be desolate, and fire shall consume the tabernacles of bribery. [Job 15:33-35]

Though none of us like brutes, hypocrites, liars, fools and the lazy, you can appreciate the reality that we are all that way at least some of the time. But fortunately, we no longer have the attitude that such conditions are of the work of the devil and can be flayed away through mortification of the flesh.

Today, when a homophobic politician or minister turns out to be secretly gay, as is all too often the case, we just nod our heads, like we knew all along that he was repressing *something*. We accept that no one is immune from projecting their own issues onto others. But projection, like repression, is a psychological term that is recent in human culture, unknown to our Biblical forebearers. Both terms assume that humans act from motivations that may be hidden, stored somewhere below the everyday conscious mind, in the unconscious mind.

But does the unconscious actually exist? For all the popularity of terms like "subconscious" and "repression," it might surprise you to know that the existence of the unconscious mind is still subject to debate. Behaviorist psychologists and others often feel the term is overly mystical in that it relates to something that cannot be seen—a bit like God. After all, since the very nature of the mind is consciousness, then an *unconscious* mind is a bit of a contradiction in terms. You may feel that the debate is simply academic, but it does have some consequences for the argument I am making, so I would like to address it right now.

What is the evidence for the existence of the unconscious mind? Actually, there are several pieces of evidence. First, there is dreams; second, the notorious "Freudian slip;" third, the nature of memory itself; and finally, fourth, hypnosis.

The first two, while plausible, are easily contested. Some researchers believe that dreams are simply random firings of the brain, a mechanism which accounts for their oddness. Attempts to impose meaning on dreams from psychological theory are nothing more than a self-fulfilling prophecy—what you look for, you find. In the end, it's not something that can be proved either way, in my opinion. Freudian slips are a little harder to explain away, but behaviorist psychologists would simply say they are random associations, and if you were to look at all slips of the tongue, Freudian slips would be a very small minority, and therefore simply coincidence.

The working of memory itself provides an interesting clue to the existence of the unconscious mind, and a useful perspective on how it works. Many introductory psychology texts note that memory recall does not work in a linear way. That is to say, when trying to remember something, referring to the past often fails, while moving on and letting the mind go on to something else often results in a resurfacing of the memory, almost as if unbidden. It is actually quite the opposite of the way a computer works when retrieving data. While behavioral psychologists would not accept this nonlinearity as a proof, it does seem almost as if another intelligence exists under the surface, one that performs best when not bothered by the conscious mind. In any case, the insight this provides is that the unconscious works best when the conscious mind is not trying, another reminder that "trying" is often counter-productive.

Hypnosis, though, is the phenomenon that provides the best proof of the existence of the unconscious mind. And it is the direct progenitor of psychotherapy itself.

FROM HYPNOSIS TO PSYCHOTHERAPY: A BRIEF HISTORY

Hypnosis was discovered by Franz Mesmer in the 18th century. The following explanation, based on information found on Bryn Mawr University's *Serendip* website, provides a good background.

In 1766, the 32-year-old Franz Anton Mesmer completed his medical training at the University of Vienna with a dissertation on the influence of the planets on human disease – a topic that would be laughed at today as mere astrology. A few years later, a young woman named Oesterlin consulted Doctor Mesmer for a recurring physical ailment. At first, in the spirit of his dissertation, Mesmer tried to relate the woman's symptoms with tidal fluctuations, but on July 28, 1774, he decided to induce an "artificial tide" by asking her to swallow a solution of iron particles while attaching magnets to her stomach and legs.

The results were to change history. Frau Oesterlin's symptoms began immediately to disappear, and with continued treatment, she recovered completely. His fame quickly spread.

In 1774, he left Vienna for Paris where he established a lucrative practice in magnetic healing and wrote a book on "animal magnetism." Influenced by the work of Benjamin Franklin and others on electricity, Mesmer developed what was for the period a reasonable explanation of the magnetic cure. He theorized that electromagnetic currents coursed through the bodies of all animals, which in fact was soon "proved" by Galvani in 1780 in his famous experiments with electricity in which he made frog legs twitch.

Unfortunately by 1785, after several well-publicized failures and the publication of a scientific expose that concluded that the evidence in favor of the existence of mesmeric fluid was insufficient, Mesmer left Paris in disgrace. He lived the remainder of his life in relative obscurity.

Though Mesmer disappeared from history his ideas lived on through a series of disciples' experiments. First, the Marquis de Puysegur, a wealthy landowner in 1788 experimented with magnetic healing by among other things inducing a "somnambulistic" trance in one of his servants. The servant who would never confided in the lord of the manor, admitted in "magnetic sleep" to a quarrel with his sister. Puysegur suggested that he resolve it upon waking, which the servant immediately did, but without any memory of the suggestion. This, now known as *post-hypnotic suggestion*, is for us, the proof of a part of the mind not apparent to the conscious mind.

But it was not until 1843, when an Englishman by the name of James Braid published a book on what he called "nervous sleep," in which he re-conceptualized how mesmerism worked that we came to our present understanding. Early in his career, he had witnessed a stage demonstration by a Swiss mesmerist that convinced him of the reality of mesmerism. After his own private experimentation, Braid came to the conclusion that the physical effects of mesmerism were actually produced by "... a condition of the nervous system, induced by a fixed and abstracted attention ..." and not through the mediation of any special agency passing from the body of the operator to that of the subject. To distinguish his views sharply from those of mesmerism, he named this state of what he identified as nervous sleep *hypnotism*, and substituted the patient's fixation on a luminous object for the mesmerists' "magnetic passes."

Braid's linking hypnotic phenomena to brain physiology, development of a straightforward and less mystical induction technique, and introduction of a terminology that was more acceptable to the medical and scientific establishment all helped prepare the way for the eventual use of hypnosis in research on psychopathology.

The final step was provided by Jean-Martin Charcot who received his M.D. in Paris in 1853. In 1862, he was appointed resident doctor at the Salpêtrière Clinic. There he created what was to become the world's most influential center for research in neurology. In 1878, Charcot was placed in charge of a ward containing women suffering from convulsions, and he set out to distinguish between convulsions that were epileptic in origin and those that were "hysterical," or in modern terms, psychological. Charcot began to employ hypnosis and discovered that under hypnosis, he could reproduce not only hysterical symptoms (such as amnesia, inability to speak, numbness) but even post-traumatic phenomena such as paralysis. This led him to group together hypnotic, hysterical, and post-traumatic phenomena, and distinguish them from those organic symptoms that arise from lesions in the brain. From this, he suggested the existence of unconscious fixations at the core of certain neuroses, a theory that eventually had a considerable influence on Freud.

In 1893, Freud and his mentor Josef Breuer published their seminal paper on the case of a woman hysteric called Anna O. The alleviation of Anna O's symptoms occurred only as the patient, under hypnosis, provided Breuer in reverse chronological order with an account of the exact circumstances under which each symptom appeared. Only when she had traced the final symptom back to the traumatic circumstances of its occurrence was she cured. Anna O's cure by this "cathartic" method, which involved bringing the trauma to consciousness and allowing it to discharge through affect, words, and guided associations, has often been seen, and was thought by Freud, to be the starting point for psychoanalysis.

While Freud, through chance, did not achieve much attention at the time, his break-out book published in 1899, *The Interpretation of Dreams*, fully incorporated the idea of the unconscious as the source of dreams, as well as the source of motivations and drives.

Sales of Freud's *Interpretation of Dreams* started slowly but within a few years changed the way we looked at ourselves. No longer could we be confident that our manners, and indeed our very civilization, was anything more than a veneer to cover over the brutish, lustful, ignorant, and fearful side of us that was no better than savage. For the inhabitants of imperialistic Europe in the Victorian era, it was like saying that under the skin, civilized Europeans were no different than tribal Africans or any other "primitive" people, as was explored in Joseph Conrad's classic novel of the time, *Heart of Darkness*.

For our purposes now, however, it is sufficient to say that Freud's ideas revealed the human psyche to be dramatically less "linear" than expected, where inputs create uncertain and possibly opposite outputs. A person seeking to discipline him or herself through extreme means might well be more likely to create a backlash, rather than the benefits he or she seeks. In fact, what Freud did was put an end to the building block notion of human improvement once and for all – (though still not understood by self-improvement books) and revealed a process in which revolution for good or ill was equally or more likely than evolution.

THE UNCONSCIOUS: MINEFIELD AND TREASURE TROVE

Freud's idea of the non-linearity of the mind, however, has never been absorbed by much of the religious, spiritual or self-improvement communities. Priests still practice celibacy, New-Agers do visualization, and pop psychologists and business consultants make lists of seven habits for this and that. They all act as if character-building happened in an orderly fashion, block by block. In fact, the truth was that the result of such discipline might instead collapse the wall, and that indeed, collapsing the wall intentionally (catharsis), might be important in curing problems.

I believe that this linearity is the fundamental mistake in self-improvement- it's a fossilized cultural artifact that's at least partially incorrect and may well have outlived its usefulness. It certainly inhibits the greater understanding of the human being's mind, spirit and emotions. Put another way, the unconscious is a minefield that needs to be navigated, or else it will undermine people's goals and intentions. At the same time, if it is understood, it could possibly contain hints or even treasures.

Psychologist Carl Jung's view was the latter. His view of archetypes suggested a richness that could be found by embodying certain aspects of the unconscious. But that is a topic I will leave unexplored, except to say that Jung viewed the unconscious as much a treasure map as a minefield. I will bring in a concept of Jung's, *synchronicity*, in the next chapter. Both views are likely valid, and to be sure, Jung as a former disciple of Freud was quite aware of both sides.

From Freud's perspective, the unconscious was a chaotic mass of infantile and primitive drives. Primary among them were lust and anger, which he conceived of as instinctive forces of creativity and destruction, or *eros* and *thanatos*. These forces were thwarted by the powerful influence of parents and society that demanded their repression. Nevertheless, they sought outlet through dreams, fantasy, and obsession. Specific memories of traumatic experiences wherein shocking experiences that couldn't be consciously processed were hidden were also stored in the unconscious. These forces and experiences could be unconsciously triggered by later events or consciously by hypnosis or therapy.

Fritz Perls later gave a more explicit explanation by showing in particular how these hidden traumas threw the whole psychological structure off balance. In his view, a person's psychological structure was analogous to a person's physical structure. For example, an injury to the foot could cause a person to favor it, so as not to use it and re-stimulate the pain, thus throwing his or her back out of place. Similarly, a psychological trauma could cause an imbalance in the psyche.

For now, it's important to simply see that the psychological paradigm shows individual human suffering is produced by three things: 1) by a generalized state of suffering through repression, and 2) by negative self image, and 3) through self-sabotage triggered by unconscious mechanisms and drives.

Self-sabotage is especially interesting. It is my contention that self sabotage, though annoying and even excruciatingly so, is a mechanism that is inevitable, and sometimes even useful. From Perl's perspective, you can see that continued adaptive responses might only end up more and more limiting an organism, in the same way that continued scar tissue would end up more and more restricting the movement of the organism. Or to use a different example, sometimes the bone must be re-broken to reset it. Therefore self-sabotage can be seen as a symptom of persistence of injury or of improper healing, reminding the organism that something is still not right.

I propose that that task of any system designed to reduce psychological suffering must address all three of these issues from the psychological paradigm. In addition, it must also address what is the usually inevitable source of suffering for humans as a whole, the vicissitudes of life, which I have brought up in Chapter 3 on happiness and will discuss again in Chapter 7.

But before I do, there are two significant aspect of Freud's theory which are important to our discussion. First, an answer to the question posed earlier as to why a person would personalize a painful occurrence by giving it a broader meaning, something that happens when people store their beliefs about life, God or themselves in their unconscious along with memories of painful events. Second, it seems likely sabotage of the unconscious mind is yet another reason that renders most straightforward attempts at self-improvement at worst futile, and at best uneven.

The implications for Epictetus are sobering, but all is not lost. In fact, there are a couple of saving graces, both from below and from above. By below I mean from within the unconscious through therapy, and from above I mean the mind and spirit of the individual. In this chapter, of course, I will limit the discussion to the former, but will take up the latter in the next.

THE RISE OF PSYCHOANALYSIS

At first, Sigmund Freud was quite optimistic about the prospect of human change. The case of Anna O. seemed to portend huge potential for change. Another early case, that of Dora, provided even more hope in a completely different way.

Dora was the pseudonym given by Freud to a patient whom he diagnosed with hysteria, whose real name was Ida Bauer. Her main hysterical symptom was *aphonia*, the loss of ability to vocalize. Ida was a nanny for the children of a married couple referred to as Herr and Frau K. The wife, Frau K, was having a love affair with Ida's father, and (according to Ida, and believed by Freud), Herr K. himself had repeatedly propositioned Ida, beginning when she was 14 years old.

Ultimately, Freud saw Ida as repressing a desire for her father, a desire for Herr K, and a desire for Frau K., as well. After only 11 weeks, Ida broke off her therapy, much to Freud's disappointment. He saw this as his failure as an analyst and decided the whole treatment had failed.

After some time, however, Ida returned to see Freud and explained how her symptoms had mostly cleared. Freud had been the only person to believe her regarding the advances of Herr K. and her father's infidelity. After the analysis, Ida chose to confront her tormentors (her father, his lover, and his lover's husband). When confronted, they confessed that she had been right all along, and after this most of her symptoms had cleared.

Freud used this case to develop his theory of infantile sexuality and the Oedipus complex. In later decades, his interpretation was criticized, because prior to it, Freud had believed nearly all of his hysteria patients had been molested, while after it, he believed the opposite.

At the time however, it gave Freud hope that even his apparent failures might be not so much due to his or his theories inadequacies, but to the power of the patient's psychological defense mechanisms. Freud published it as a case entitled, "Dora, Fragments of an Analysis of a Case of Hysteria" in 1905.

WHAT DREAMS MAY COME

As I mentioned, it was nevertheless Freud's book on dream analysis, *The Interpretation of Dreams,* published in 1899 that exposed his ideas to the largest public audience. It took four years for the initial printing of 600 copies to sell out, but sales increased every year thereafter. It is hard to consider today just how influential the book was and how convincing, but back then it went through over a dozen editions within Freud's lifetime and remains in print to this very day.

Early in the book Freud makes clear that unlike in other "dream books," going back to the ancient Greeks (and still available even now), in his book there is no "decoding" of dreams, meaning no "this can be translated into that," and no prediction can be made of the future. But even without that meaning to dreams, Freud maintains that the folksy beliefs of the masses are "nearer the truth than the skepticism of scientists." Nevertheless, Freud is clear that the direction of dream analysis is backwards into the dreamer's past, and the deciphering of the dream is a rigorous and tenuous process which demands a high and almost unattainable degree of objectivity.

The dream he offers first is the now famous dream of July, 23-24, 1895, known as "Irma's Injection." He then spends the next ten pages analyzing the dream line by line. Freud's intention was to nip scientific skepticism in the bud, by not only proving the dream was meaningful, but that *everything* in the dream could be understood. At the end of the analysis, he steps back and offers an overview: *"The dream represents a certain state of affairs as being as I would wish it to be: its content is thus a wish-fulfillment, its motive a wish.* The next page or so explains how that insight reveals the meaning of many of the obscure symbols in the dream, and he concludes the chapter by reiterating: *"After the work of interpretation has been completed, the dream reveals itself as a wish-fulfillment.* (authors italics)

Wish fulfillment is the essence of Freud's theory, and as I mentioned earlier, perhaps its most controversial issue. A comparison of the first and later editions of *Interpretation of Dreams* shows it originally to be devoid of many of the easy sexual interpretations now associated with Freudian theory, such as stairs signifying intercourse or a table representing women. These kinds of interpretations turn out to have been the result of Freud's later association with psychoanalyst Wilhelm Stekel.

But in a way, wish fulfillment is an even more shocking doctrine than any overly sexual interpretations.

Understand this: Wish fulfillment is *not just* saying your dream is about sex with your mother or killing your father, but that you *wanted* to do it. This, of course, is the now famous *Oedipus Complex* that Freud made famous and which he introduces gently as the result of introspection into his own dreams.

The shocking nature of wish fulfillment is then shown to be the very reason *why* we dream and why our dreams are so distorted. Dreams, Freud believed, occur as a safety valve for unattainable wishes, and those wishes are disguised so as to preserve sleep. That is to say, like fantasies and daydreams, dreams at night provide an outlet for desires that cannot be fulfilled, keeping the dreamer from going mad. Fantasies that are too shocking for the conscious mind (killing your father, sex with your mother, etc.) can only be put forward while the mind is asleep.

I mention all this because the concept of wish fulfillment is Freud's way of relating to my happiness equation, by saying "wanting to get what we want." He is adding to mine the idea that what we want *consciously* is only part of the story, and there is another *darker* layer of wants hidden beneath the surface that drive us in unknown and unpredictable ways—in the unconscious. This tells us, I believe, that the drives to "get what we want" are a crucial part of our psyche, both consciously and unconsciously and that frustrating (i.e. not fulfilling) the unconscious drives can also be a cause of conflict or unhappiness.

But even though those unconscious drives are normally hidden, they can be known, if we follow his lead. Near the end of his book, Freud displays his genius in applying his method to what he calls *recalcitrant material*—such as elements in dreams that defy easy interpretation—and the difficult process of explaining dreams about proper names and numbers. In regards to the first, he relates an example of his own dream featuring silver paper. He realizes that one way of medically referring to such paper is *stanniol* or silver foil, which reminds him of the name "Stannius," an author of a treatise he once read and admired with awe. Note that the resolution of the meaning was twice removed from the original symbol, demonstrating free association, a technique he came to rely on.

Looking at dream numbers, Freud described a dream by one of his patients: "She wants to pay for something. Her daughter takes 3fl, 65kr (Austrian currency) from her purse; but she says: what are you doing it only costs 21kr [p. 264].

He notes that the original amount, 3fl 65kr, represent another year of treatment his patient is considering undergoing with him, and the amount of 21kr represent the number of school days her daughter has left, after which she will have less expense. You can almost see Freud smirk as he notes that the sentiment is no more complex than "time is money," the smaller sum simply representing his patient's *wish* that expenses be lessened.

In other words, like everything else, the names and numbers in a dream were only symbolic. It's hard to overstate how convincing all this was to Freud's readers. Even reading *The Interpretation of Dreams* today, one can't help being impressed. Freud dream analysis demonstrated that the most irrational part of the human mind could be explained scientifically. And if it could be understood, perhaps it could be changed.

Many flocked to Vienna to study under Freud, as well as become his patients. Other intellectuals applied his theories to literature and some even combined it with Marxism to create a philosophy of social and political liberation.

But as we realize now, some of the optimism was overstated. Over the long term, some of Freud's patients regressed, and others had frustratingly slow progress. Many of his students left to form their own schools of psychotherapy. Even when they include dream analysis, wish fulfillment is now seen by many as only one aspect of dreams. This is not to say that people had not been helped. Many people continued to go to analysts for short or longer periods and benefited from guidance, counseling, or just having an objective person available so they could vocalize their issues.

In truth, it was probably never as popular as it seemed. The high price was probably prohibitive to outside the upper and upper middle classes. But it is worthwhile to examine the strengths and weaknesses of the practice as it turned out.

PROS AND CONS

What psychoanalysis and its followers achieved was not insubstantial. There were improvements in most cases, if not always cures. The pressures of unconscious drives were lessened for many patients. There was a tremendous increase in the understanding of the mind, and the beginning of studying mental and emotional states on a scientific basis. The harshness of our society's judgments on mental problems also lessened as we finally had a rational means of understanding them. But by the 1960s, the glory period of the "four or five sessions a week" Freudian analysis had passed.

In general, not to dismiss Freud, research has shown that nearly all schools of therapy are equally successful. What seems to work is not the theory but the therapist. And what seems to work with therapists is their ability to perform or enable a few fundamental processes, such as *attention*, *empathy* and *transference*. All of these allow the patient a greater amount of self-acceptance and distance to reduce the pressure of the unconscious on the personality.

But the limitations of therapy also seem clear when you take into account the following:

1. The personality is largely formed by adulthood; therefore the most lasting changes will be at the margins rather than at the core.
2. Psychoanalysis turned out to be too long and too expensive, an issue that was addressed teaching people to counsel each other (as in by the Re-Evaluation Counseling movement) but mostly by therapists simple scaling back the amount of treatment time.
3. Psychoanalysis ignored the philosophical side of happiness and depression, as laid out long ago by Epictetus
4. It failed to account for the biological side of mental illness (a later development of scientific medicine)
5. It ignored the spiritual side of the individual.

So while psychotherapy could reduce the pressure on the personality, it did not seem to eliminate that pressure enough to truly and predictably help many individuals.

For our purposes in this book, though, the discussion has demonstrated a large part of the difficulty with self-improvement and self-help solutions, which is the presence of unconscious motivations that cause us to act out in unpredictable ways and the working of self-sabotage—both of which are deep-seated and extremely difficult to root out. Not only that, it should be clear by now that forms of mental control such as positive thinking and even Epictetus cannot touch or even *get close* to touching the contents of the deep unconscious.

Freud's (and my) focus on dreams also has supported another point: Dreams are at their root not unlike ordinary thoughts. They are made up of wish fulfillments and anxieties – the things we want and don't want. Freud suggests that we shouldn't blame ourselves for the content of our dreams. Surely, we wouldn't blame a pet, when we see it twitch as it dreams of chasing or being chased. Likewise, he teaches us to see that even our violent and sexual dreams, wish fulfillment or not, as not reflecting our true worth, because they are generated in a place far beneath our control. Perhaps, then, we can start to see that the content of our thoughts also are beyond value judgment.

But by the late 1960s, in any case, a consensus was starting to emerge that psychotherapy had not fully lived up to its promise, and two new trends began to appear. For psychiatrists, who were trained as MDs, the promise of new drugs that could attack mental illness on its biochemical basis was alluring. But for the non-medical psychologists and therapists, the trend was split between behaviorists who preferred to ignore the unconscious in favor of simply conditioning and modifying behavior, and humanists who preferred to concentrate on the emotions and even the spirit.

It is to the spirit I now turn my attention, moving on from psychology to explore religion and spirituality as they pertain to understanding and finding happiness, the subject of the next chapter.

In transition, I leave you with the following historical tidbit. In 1961, psychologist Michael Murphy and a friend co-founded Esalen at the hot springs in Big Sur, California. Their vision was for a open-ended exploration of human consciousness, based on Murphy's understanding of meditation and psychology. Among their earliest lecturers was our friend Alan Watts, an ex-Episcopal priest, philosopher, and writer who had followed his early bestseller on the meaning of happiness with a number of books popularizing Zen Buddhism. Numbered among the other early lecturers were Harvard psychologists Timothy Leary and Richard Alpert, who had both gained notoriety with their experimentation with psychedelic drugs. Alpert, as you may know if you are a certain age, soon dropped out and went to India, changing his name to Ram Dass and becoming a spiritual leader for the new hippie generation.

It is hard to overstate the impact of Esalen and other places of exploration as the leading edge of American psychology began to turn Eastward. It was as if some of the best and brightest minds in psychology had decided that Freud's impulse towards a modern science of unconscious was a dead end, and the ancient wisdom of India and China presented a better chance at solving the problems of living.

CHAPTER 5

TURNING EAST

What does the world of spirituality and religion offer in our examination of how to live and to reduce unhappiness? If the reality of the unconscious is proven by the existence of hypnosis, is there any evidence for the reality of the other invisible side of human life, the one debated by philosophers for centuries—the existence of a spiritual force, even God him or herself?

In this chapter, I would like to follow the path of the Esalen psychologists in their turn Eastward and discuss spirituality as we conceive of it currently, and how this affects the probabilities for happiness.

JOURNEY TO THE EAST

In 1932, German author Herman Hesse penned a novel entitled *Journey to the East.* Later, in the 1960s, the novelist was suddenly popular again as Eastern spirituality became mainstream, not just among the therapeutic movement but among young people, students, and intellectuals. Hesse's novels, like *Siddhartha*, *Narcissus and Goldmund*, and *Steppenwolf* told the stories of spiritual exploration in different places and times. But *Journey to the East* was probably his most explicit rendering of his views of a spiritual quest.

Back in the '70s, led by the therapists at Esalen, a generation of us joined a real life experiential "journey to the East," and what we found was a lot to like, and eventually, some things to debunk. These are the subjects I will explore in the next two chapters, which focus on spirituality and how I see its link to living well and the question of happiness.

Although my personal spiritual quest during that time stayed mostly inside the U.S., I took one trip to the East as a vacation, but it was one that had a very interesting incident relevant to our discussion here.

BALI BELLY

Bali, Indonesia: Slumped in the back seat of the car, I was holding my stomach and watching the tops of palm trees and jungle foliage whiz by. One side of my face was pressed against the vinyl seat back, and my hand pressed against my aching and gurgling stomach as I tried to massage it as best I could. My head throbbed, and I felt dizzy and nauseous. Out the corner of the window, I watched as we passed wooden carts, bicycles and rice fields. I was sick to my stomach and suddenly very worried. It was 1990. I was in Bali on vacation with my family.

My mind ran through some of the events of the past few days as I weakly pondered my situation. Before I'd left the U.S. a week before, an acquaintance made an unusual request. He'd learned that unlike the rest of Indonesia, which was Muslim, Bali was Hindu, and he wanted know if there were any of what he referred to as "Krishna gurus" in Bali. I was skeptical, because I thought he was referring to Hare Krishnas dancing in airports as they used to do in '70s and figured it was strictly an American phenomenon. But I promised I would look into it.

One evening, after a day lounging at my hotel pool and walking through the Monkey Forest in Ubud, I decided to visit the local bookstore. I had seen no evidence of either any Hare Krishnas or gurus, but once inside the bookstore, I decided to see what I could find. I soon found a small guidebook entitled *Religion in Bali*.

The book quickly disabused me of any hope of satisfying my friend's wish, since it turned out that Balinese were Shaivites, a branch of Hinduism with a different diety, Lord Shiva. Furthermore, the Balinese had a sweet but quaint aversion to religious leaders and asceticism, and so the normal Hindu preoccupation with gurus and yogis was pretty much absent, except for among Westerners. Although each home had three shrines and many others scattered through the town, spiritual practice in Bali was mainly limited to placing offerings on every doorstep in the morning, and at the many temples at various times of the day. Typically, these offerings consisted of flowers, and sometimes cigarettes and coins. The offerings are quite numerous, and, as it is considered bad form to step on one, clumsy Westerners must be very careful to avoid offending the spirits and those who make them offerings.

I did find out that there were a few Hindus in Bali who were not Shaivites, a sect of mostly priests who were devotees of Lord Vishnu and performed rituals for psychic protection. They were also notable for their opposition to the caste system, which, though weaker than in India, still existed in Bali.

I found this most intriguing. From some inquiries at my hotel, I found out that a practicing priest lived in a neighboring village. I hired a car and driver and set off to visit. The priest, on whom I had dropped in on unannounced, welcomed me cordially, and after talking to me for some time, introduced me to his family and invited me in for tea. He was a thin fellow in his 50s, dressed in a dark headdress with the checkered sash popular in Bali. His son was also thin but dressed in a western style of white shirt and dark trousers. Our conversation ranged widely. He told me he was called on to dedicate homes and banish the occasional evil spirit through a special ceremony. My final question was right up his alley, "What is the best form of psychic protection?"

He answered in a characteristically Balinese way, "To see Good and Evil as one." The emblem of the island is a black and white checkered flag symbolizing balance of good and evil.

On the drive home, I started to feel some intestinal queasiness, locally known as "Bali belly," a Westerner's reaction to the unfamiliar germs of the area found in insufficiently boiled water. Apparently, the evil spirits of bacteria had not been completely banished in the priest's presence. Since my father had just a few years before been hospitalized with amoebic dysentery after a trip to a third world country, I got very worried.

I closed my eyes and offered a silent prayer to whoever was listening that I somehow not get sick. When I opened my eyes, I saw an old Toyota pickup truck passing us on the road. As I watched, I noticed that where the tailgate should have had the name Toyota, in official-looking, large letters was painted the word, GARLIC.

I thought, *Oh ... Garlic... that would work...* I asked the driver if there was a street market in the next village. He responded there was, and I asked him to take me there. I quickly found a stall selling garlic and bought about ten cloves, along with a large box of crackers from the next stall. I ate crackers and raw garlic for the next hour, until all the bugs in my belly were dead.

Looking back, I later realized that it was not only odd that the truck saying GARLIC had passed us at the exact instant I was "praying," but that the word was written in English at all, instead of in Indonesian, which was "bawang putih." It is also odd that someone would have painted out TOYOTA and painted in GARLIC in the first place. I should also mention that as far as I could see, the truck was not carrying any garlic. That someone had years before painted out TOYOTA and replaced it with GARLIC on a truck for God knows what reason, and in English, and that

GARLIC appeared exactly when needed, all seems a bit too much to be explained by coincidence.

SYNCHRONICITY

Carl Jung felt that the best evidence of a spiritual force is the phenomenon of *synchronicity*. He coined the term as an explanation for how oracles such as the *I Ching* or astrology could work. The basic notion is that everything is interconnected and that changes in one place are reflected in changes elsewhere.

Jung proposed synchronicity as an alternative to the conventional notion of cause and effect, which emphasizes a simple cause having a limited and knowable effect. Instead, with synchronicity, things move holistically, one affecting one another. The closest thing to this in science is the popularization of Chaos Theory in the 1990s, which famously stated that the flapping of a butterfly's wings in one country could cause a hurricane in another. Jung, however, would have said that neither the hurricane nor the butterfly caused each other, but instead they were an interconnected part of a greater whole. And further than that, Chaos Theory stated, watching some part of that whole could give information about another part.

A similar line of reasoning has arisen in the New Age version of quantum theory. While I have serious reservations about this current interpretation, I will simply say that the notion of *quantum entanglement* states something very similar to Jung's concept. In its simplest form, quantum entanglement means that information can be known *non-locally*. The concept of Bell's inequality principle in physics is an example of that.

Going back to Jung, Henri Ellenberger gives the example of a woman patient of Jung's whose analysis was not progressing well because of her inability to let go due to an excess of rationality. According to the story related in Ellenberger's *The Discovery of the Unconscious*, the woman had dreamed of a golden beetle that was given to her and was discussing it with Jung, when a beetle flew into the room. Jung picked it up and presented it to her. She was so impressed by this incident of synchronicity, that for the first time in her life she put aside her armor of rationality.

MODERN DAY SPIRITUALITY

In the modern era, spirituality is not restricted to *received* religion, meaning the religion from one's upbringing -- as opposed to a faith developed from personal experience or revelation. Although fundamentalism and traditionalism are stronger than ever in many parts of the world, they have in a sense been reduced to a cultural defense mechanism, a reaction against individualism and changing times. This observation has been made in various ways over the last 50 years, notably in Clifford Geertz's *Islam Observed* in 1960 and Benjamin Barber's *Jihad Vs Mc World* in 1993.

The leading edge of religious/spiritual thought, although much mocked, has for several decades now probably been from the Eastern-influenced New Age and related movements. Even such mainstream venues as corporate and government trainings have been heavily influenced by New Age concepts and activities. And nothing can match the huge influence of the Oprah Winfrey Show on her tens of millions of viewers in its 20-year television run. Compared to previous generations, there are no modern counterparts to the 20th century religious philosophers, such as Karl Barth, Teilhard de Chardin, and Martin Buber in the modern mainstream.

Indeed, those greats have been largely replaced by atheists like Richard Dawkins and Christopher Hitchens in modern thought. Yet it might be wrong to think of atheism as anything other than a revulsion against the current extremes of fundamentalism in political discourse rather than a new intellectual stream. That is to say, the critique by atheism was begun over a hundred years ago and little has been added to it in its modern version, except perhaps in

Dawkins' case, whose books such as *The God Delusion* have grounded it more in neurological science.

So far, the model I have built is perhaps more than a little pessimistic. I have shown that our feelings are heavily dependent on factors that are often out of our control. Epictetus pointed to that two thousand years ago, and counseled a philosophy of restraint and sober thinking. But I have shown that our modern understanding has made things even worse in two ways: First, by briefly noting how it is more difficult to discern nowadays what is within our control, and more significantly, by showing that our ability to live according to philosophies, rules, or even good ideas is substantially threatened by what we now know about our thinking, emotions, and subconscious processes.

However, all may not be lost. We constantly see on the shelves of bookstores, on TV shows and in motivational seminars that a spiritual approach can literally offer some help from above. What I intend to do in the remainder of this chapter is explore how that spirituality works, and why spirituality may be necessary, but also why not to put too much faith in the spiritual approach alone.

INTERIOR AWARENESS

A recent article in *Scientific American* by Dr. Emma Seppala, Associate Director at the Center for Compassion and Altruism Research and Education, presents some interesting evidence on the existence of what she terms *interior awareness*.

> *Most of us prioritize externally-oriented attention. When we think of attention, we often think of focusing on something outside of ourselves. We "pay attention" to work, the TV, our partner, traffic, or anything that engages our senses. However, a whole other world exists that most of us are far less aware of: an internal world, with its varied landscape of emotions, feelings, and sensations.*

> *Yet it is often the internal world that determines whether we are having a good day or not, whether we are happy or unhappy. That is why we can feel angry despite beautiful surroundings or feel perfectly happy despite being stuck in traffic. For this reason perhaps, this newly discovered pathway of attention may hold the key to greater well-being.*

Seppala goes on to say that although interior sensations predominate in infants, by adulthood, we become distracted by the dominance of exterior stimulation, so much so that our own internal feelings and reactions often startle or surprise us. She writes: "A flush of anger, a choked up feeling of sadness, or the warmth of love in our chest often appear to come out of the blue."

Seppala doesn't discuss what it is in the internal world that is causing these internal feelings, but from our earlier discussion, it is clear they would be reactions to our thoughts about the past and future, as well as unattended-to feelings.

Seppala reports research by Bernard Farb at the University of Toronto that is contrary to decades of belief that all attention is the same and originates in the pre-frontal lobe of the brain. Farb showed that the prefrontal cortex may indeed be specialized for attending to external information, while older and more buried parts of the brain, including the *insula* and *posterior cingulate cortex,* appear to be specialized in observing our internal "landscape." This older brain's internal awareness seemed to work by directly tapping into a bodily awareness that was free from social judgment or conceptual self-evaluation, according to the researchers. Put another way, this internal awareness was both calmer and more objective than external awareness.

Significantly, Seppala writes:

> *These findings {of Farb} have important implications for emotional well-being. States of mind such as anxiety, depression, and anger often engage the prefrontal cortex. "I can't shut my mind off"—a*

statement most of us can relate to in times of stress. Have you ever tried to talk yourself out of such a state of high stress and failed? Trying to talk ourselves out of being less anxious or angry is often a futile exercise. The mind quite simply has a hard time telling itself what to do.

By now, you are familiar with this phenomenon, having already been introduced to Daniel Wegner's idea of *ironic processes* earlier in this book. Seppala felt that Farb's findings, however, suggest that the brain's wiring which produces interior awareness may provide a built-in system separate from the conscious mind that helps produce calm states. She writes, "We can't control our mind with our mind (or our pre-frontal cortex with the pre-frontal cortex), but with *introceptive* awareness, we may be able to escape our racing thoughts. The expression "take a deep breath" in a moment of anger or fear is a common saying that directly taps into our ability to use our *introceptive* awareness."

Interestingly, other research reported in Seppala's article by University of California researcher Jocelyn Szc found that even professional dancers, who presumably had substantial body awareness, were less able to tap into interior awareness than were meditators. This shows that internal awareness is not the same as body awareness, but something distinct.

Seppala concluded that this interior awareness might be the solution to the ironic process dilemma posed by Wegner.

What I believe is a little more complicated. I think it is speculative and probably wishful thinking to suppose that a little interior awareness practiced for short periods daily, or "as needed," is sufficient to defeat the power of ironic processes, which, after all, seems based on primary brain functions. Moreover, the power of the unconscious structure of the psyche as outlined by Freud probably account for an even deeper anchoring of those processes in the personality. So based on all the reasons I have outlined in the book, I think ironic processes are simply too strong. Perhaps over a lifetime, meditation could erase the control of ironic processes, but then again, maybe not. As Jack Kornfield described in his book, *A Path With Heart*, years of ten-hours-a-day meditation in Thailand did not prepare him for dealing with work and relationships on his return to America. However, the simple existence of *some* process that aids us is significant, because frankly we need all the help we can get. So with that caveat, I think it is worthwhile to pursue it.

How does this "interior awareness" work? There are a couple of ways: First by giving you greater awareness of your body, it allows the mind to consciously regulate your body. Breathing exercises and meditation are known ways to deliberately relax and reduce stress. Second, by moving your attention away from the exterior world and into the interior, you are also producing what was described in Chapter 3 on emotions: distance. Literally, the stimuli of the outer world seem farther away and less important as you bring your attention inward.

In addition, I suggest that interior awareness is precisely what makes the operation of synchronicity possible and noticeable to the human mind, allowing us to pick up some extra help literally from "outside" ourselves, as well as from the deepest parts within. Put another way, the ability to momentarily let go of exterior awareness and the intensity of its focus is probably what allows the mind to be drawn to the synchronicities that are all around. My "Bali belly" episode illustrated this with the appearance of GARLIC on a truck that led to my cure.

INTERIOR AWARENESS AND SYNCHRONICITY

Let me give another example. One sunny Sunday morning, I had parked near the pier in Santa Barbara and was enjoying the weekly craft show along the beach walk. It was a gorgeous, cloudless summer morning, and there were many booths to browse and enjoy. After an hour or so, I began to get hungry. It was so beautiful, I didn't feel like heading home to fix breakfast, so I crossed the street and got an outside table at a cafe right on Cabrillo Blvd. After

I finished my breakfast, I dallied for a long while drinking coffee and reading the Sunday *Los Angeles Times*. Suddenly, the waiter came over and rudely grabbed the umbrella shading my table, and moved it to a table where a couple had just sat down. I had already gotten my check, so my first thought was simply, *That must mean it's time to go.*

But then I thought how rude and abrupt it was that the waiter had taken my umbrella without even an apology or explanation. I considered moving, but then decided just to pay my check. At the cash register, I also considered complaining about the waiter, since I thought it might be good feedback about his customer service. After a moment, I shrugged it off and left the café, crossing the street to my car, where a parking lady was just pulling up to give me a ticket. I had forgotten I was in a 90-minute zone. Had I slowed for even another 30 seconds to comment about the incident, I would have gotten a $30 ticket.

My first thought was simply relief that I had left the café so promptly. But as is my nature, I soon started to reflect on the meaning of the incident. The waiter taking the umbrella was a kind of synchronicity that had saved me $30. But if God or whoever had been willing to intercede on such a small incident, why hadn't He done so on the many bigger mistakes in my life? *What was up with that?*

I came up with a couple possible explanations. The first was that perhaps God was at all times trying to protect me, but I had missed His messages or allowed an emotional reaction to prevent me from acting on them. That was a pretty depressing thought. The other, explanation, which was even more depressing in an entirely different way, was that God only acted in unimportant matters, because in the important ones it was necessary for people to learn their lessons.

I tossed these ideas around for the better part of the day as I was going through my errands. Finally, I opted to split the difference, as I usually do when two alternatives seem reasonable. It seems likely that guidance is available in all situations. But since learning is often done through making mistakes, it is often the case that we need to be allowed to make them, so whichever choice we make, there is some benefit.

In any case, it seems likely that there are many synchronicities that we miss because of our getting caught up in external awareness or internal obsessions. Thinking about the number of minor car accidents I have had over my lifetime and the even greater number of near misses, I can say with a high degree of certainty that every one of the accidents occurred when I was preoccupied with something. One even happened when I was concentrating on backing out of a blind parking place, trying to make sure I didn't pull in front of another car. Another person coming from the opposite direction backed into me!

On the other hand, all the near misses occurred when I was driving in a relaxed fashion. Somehow my foot hit the brake, or I took an unusual evasive action, even before I was aware of the threat. So to reiterate another time, this relaxed internal awareness, while it may or may not be strong enough to solve the problem of ironic processes, is an extremely beneficial one, in that it allows one, to use the popular phrase, to more easily "let go and let God."

PERCEPTION AND MISPERCEPTION

There is one final benefit to having an interior awareness that was not mentioned in Seppala's article, which the following bit of history illustrates.

Early in the 20th century, philosopher Edmund Husserl began to question the assumptions of mathematics and science. Although trained as a mathematician, he fell in love with philosophy under the tutelage of Franz Brentano, the German philosopher who introduced psychology to philosophy. Brentano coined the phrase "Perception is misperception," which meant that our bias and inevitable intentions towards an external object inevitably colored our perceptions. For example, a cow likely sees grass differently than a human, because the former wants to eat it, while the latter wants something that looks nice for his or her lawn. A man or woman is seen differently by a lover than by a friend. Science itself is biased by its theories, which narrow the ways scientists view their subject.

Husserl went into the notions of ideas and objects at some depth, and eventually founded the philosophical school of *phenomenology* with his insights, influencing a generation of philosophers like Heidegger, Sartre, Merleau-Ponty, and even to some degree Carl Jung, who considered himself a phenomenological psychologist. Husserl's notion was that although a person's perception of external objects was inevitably biased, it was possible to grasp the nature of a thing by intuition and by "bracketing" one's bias, in essence, holding it aside.

Husserl was aware of Buddhism and other forms of Eastern thought, and considered his method, which he called *transcendental phenomenology*, to be parallel with Buddhist philosophy. We can see in transcendental phenomenology a rationale for the development of "interior" awareness and the related overthrow of the dominance of external awareness, which should have the effect of increasing the accuracy of external perception by reducing the bias of intentionality.

LIFE AND DEATH

Moving away from such lofty concerns, you are likely familiar with Karl Marx's famous quote, "Religion is the sigh of the oppressed creature, the heart of a heartless world, and the soul of soulless conditions. It is the opium of the people," which comes from his 1843 *Critique of Hegel's Philosophy of Right*. In this, it seems Marx was probably echoing similar words of the Marquis De Sade in *Juliette* or the philosopher Novalis whom he may have read in his youth. But the sentiment is clear. For them, religion is a "happy pill," that once downed prevents people from taking action to solve their problems.

Rodney Stark and Bill Bainbridge in their book *Future of Religion* have argued similarly. As social scientists, they agree that people generally tend to respond to life by pursuing rewards and avoiding punishments, which is what I have been saying all along: that we tend to go after what we want and avoid what we don't want. But there are some areas where rewards do not exist, they argue, most notably the inevitability of life and death or the larger social arrangements such as inequality and poverty. Here religion offers what Stark and Bainbridge call "compensators," a substitute for a reward. In other words, religion can't offer you a *real* reward for leading a moral life, but it *can* offer you a coupon, which is that you get to go to heaven. Since death is a universal phenomenon, the authors argue that religion, even though false, is inevitable because compensators, while inferior to real rewards, are better than nothing.

If you have followed my original argument that happiness is based on the expectation you will get what you want in the future, you may have noticed a possible problem. This is that as we age, we have less and less to look forward to, and more and more to fear, like illness and death. Therefore, you'd expect that as they age, people would tend to become unhappy.

In fact, that is generally true. Rates of depression are higher among the elderly, as are rates of suicide. Although general rates of suicide peak at around 45-54, rates of suicide of the elderly are roughly three times higher than that of teenagers, even though teenage suicide gets far more attention. If we limit our view to non-Hispanic white males, we find the rate of elderly suicide at more than *nine* times the rate of teenagers by age 85, according to the National Institute of Mental Health.

Why are non-Hispanic white males so much more at risk than other groups? Probably the best explanation was given in Emile Durkheim's classic work, *Suicide*, written in 1897. Looking across the entire population of Europe, he found that the degree of a society's social integration was highly correlated with a lower suicide rate. In my home state of Nevada, we have a suicide rate nearly double the national average, usually attributed to higher residential transiency. It's not the gambling, since rates in rural counties in Nevada are higher, and the rates in Nevada are exceeded by sparsely populated states like Montana and Alaska. Social isolation is more likely the cause, and one can see how greater isolation is related to people having less of what they want which may simply be friends and people to share their lives with. Also, white males for various reasons seem to have less involvement with community institutions such as churches and social groups than women and most minorities.

But let's assume for a minute that Marx, as well as Stark and Bainbridge were wrong in assuming that religion is false. In fact, Rodney Stark, who, at the time of writing his book in 1985 described himself as "incapable of religion," in 2007 called himself an "independent Christian," according to Wikipedia. And as we have seen, synchronicity has been seen as a "soft" proof of the existence of God. If so, the adoption of a spiritual perspective can have a great value in reducing unhappiness at facing death and old age, which is, after all, something we can't do much about. Instead, that perspective gives us something we *can* do, which is prepare ourselves for the afterlife, *if* we can find something we can actually believe in.

Such a spiritual perspective could actually be a source of unhappiness, if you believe you are going to hell—but if not, could be a source of comfort. The worse case scenario however, might be one in which you are sent to hell for your doubts, creating a conundrum of truly medieval proportions!

A SPIRITUAL SOLUTION?

What I have tried to do so far in this chapter is to provide a potential escape hatch from the rather gloomy predicament in which I left humanity after Chapter 4. Humans are subject to the whims of fate which buffets their happiness like a badminton birdie in a windstorm. Attempts to resolve this by simply adopting a more realistic set of expectations of life, as proposed by Epictetus, are undermined by strong emotional forces and worse, by unconscious mechanisms and sabotage. Even psychotherapy has had limited success at curing many difficult conditions.

In this chapter, I have shown that we at least have an ally in the struggle, which is our ability to go inside (interior awareness), distance ourselves from emotions, and allow ourselves to "Let go and let God." This is essentially what you learned if you watched Oprah or if you read numerous books on New Age spirituality. But unfortunately, things are never quite that simple. The forces that were addressed in the beginning of the book still arise to attack and undermine the spiritual seeker. In addition, the pursuit of spiritual awareness isn't without some pitfalls of its own. So while I am pointing to an escape hatch for our existential dilemma, I am also strongly pointing out that no one approach is a panacea, and that spiritual self-help books that do not address the earlier issues I brought up in this book are destined to fall short for most people.

Additionally, I would like to briefly throw some light on why so many of these spiritual books are full of obvious hokum. Let me start with my own experience.

When I first became aware of the potentials of spirituality, it seemed that a whole new world had opened up to me. Bookstores became treasure troves of possible spiritual adventures. Every spiritual leader I met at a workshop or event was a fount of potential wisdom as they shared with me astounding experiences and deep knowledge.

After a few months though, I began to notice some problems. Nearly everything I was told contained much disagreement. One person quoted Masters exhorting their students to strive on until they reached a stage where finding God was more important than the next breath. Another said relaxation and letting go was the path. Over and over again, I found that these spiritual leaders' advice was mutually contradictory. Furthermore, their teachings on the aspects of existence itself had little agreement. Were there seven planes of existence, or only three? Did we reincarnate as animal or only as humans? It seemed that rather than being a source of objectivity, the vast "interior awareness" these leaders had attained was a source of even greater subjectivity, where even less could be known for certain than in the plain old solid world.

Oddly, my response at the time was not to become skeptical of all claims to spiritual knowledge, but rather to decide that the point of view I'd already developed was the correct one, and all the others were false. Perhaps not so oddly, since that approach is the one most people take, one that has contributed to countless wars over countless centuries. It was only after I had tried a few different "paths" and tried to reconcile very different worldviews that I realized objectivity in spirituality was a potentiality that was rarely attained. Or as Yogi Berra famously said, "In theory, theory and practice are connected, but in practice, not so much."

Regardless, I do believe that developing my own "interior awareness" helped me in many ways, including my graduate studies, because it allowed to me grasp theories more easily by being able to just "go blank" for an instant, allowing my receptivity to let things fall into place. But I have become sensitive to the fact that even the slightest bias in thoughts or perspective can color perceptions in the rarified spiritual world.

REALITIES OF THE SPIRITUAL MARKETPLACE

At some point in my spiritual search, I, like many, decided to become more serious and get some help from a spiritual teacher. Here another can of worms presented itself. *How do I choose which teacher to follow?*

Based on my own experience and my observation of others faced with the same challenge, there are a few ways to evaluate a particular spiritual teacher. These are: The teacher's claims, testimonials, miracles, and the qualities of the students that surround the teachers. Unfortunately, there are problems with accepting the validity of any of these, as we shall see.

Obviously in the spiritual marketplace, each teacher is competing with all the others for attracting students. This leads to a devaluation of one of the most important spiritual qualities of all, which is *humility*. Every teacher must claim to be the best or risk losing their students to someone who appears to be better. It's simply another version of the "best hamburgers in town" phenomenon. The only way to know, then, is to try them out. Hopefully, Yelp.com will someday get around to posting reviews of gurus.

Which leads us to testimonials - which we frequently see on the back of book covers or on posters. All teachers seem to have them, and of course, they are all positive. If they weren't, they wouldn't get printed. So that approach is out. I guess this is as good a place as any to mention my observation about testimonials. My motto is, "Everything works a little for a lot of people, a lot for a few people, and miraculously for one or two." Those one or two are the people who write the testimonials!

And that brings us to miracles. Everyone wants them, but very few people have actually seen one, so any that do happen get played up big time. I recall an acquaintance who had a business promoting colon cleansing herbs. He wrote a book about his health business and in the final chapter told of an experience while fasting in which he had a vision of an angel. Of course, from then on, everyone who read his book wanted to cleanse their colons in order to have a vision—which is not the normal market appeal of such products.

Or there's the famous example of Werner Erhard, the founder of the legendary '70s human potential workshop called *est*. Of course, everyone wanted to know his credentials for creating such a workshop, especially when there were so many "enlightened" gurus around, so he told people he had had an enlightenment experience while driving to work across the Golden Gate Bridge. Problem solved. Hearing this, I remarked to a friend that the experience must have been pretty mild if he was able to keep control of his car the whole time!

It would seem that the requirement of extraordinary experiences and miracles for guru validity has the contrary effect of promoting fakery. This is something that many who investigated odd spiritual claims since the time of the notorious Theosophist Madame Blavatsky in the late 19th century have pointed out. She claimed to have produce materializations that came from the "ethers" where the masters resided, but were later discovered as objects coming out of trap doors or reflected in trick mirrors.

Again, the competition of the spiritual marketplace is likely to blame. Given that no one outside circle of adherents can verify the claim, why not make it bigger than everyone else's claim? Let's not just clear your seven chakras, but why not fourteen more? It doesn't matter that no one has written about that many chakras until now,—that's just because no one has seen them yet! The same is true of course with spiritual self-help books which have the added advantage of limiting your verifying their claims to simply looking at the author's picture on the back cover and guessing.

Finally, there is the possibility of assessing the quality of the spiritual students who study with the teacher. This may be a little more reliable, but hardly infallible, because a teacher can promote a desired image by requiring his followers to dress a certain way to look good or select the most attractive and relatable ones for presenting to the public.

In the end, the teacher's qualifications boil down to an internal state—their own personal state of enlightenment. Assuming that their claim is not total fiction, it bears looking into about what their enlightenment actually means—and what it does not necessarily mean - the subject of our next discussion.

NEW GURU, OLD EGO

By now, we've all heard numerous stories of gurus, spiritual teachers, ministers and priests, and the various peccadilloes they have been involved in, be it sex, drugs, money or power. When it's a minister, priest, or rabbi, part of their claim for our attention is that they have something that we do not. When it's a guru or supposedly enlightened teacher, that goes double. And yet, these spiritual leaders are hardly immune from the same problems and temptations we mere mortals face. One can be forgiven if one ends up throwing out the baby with the bath water, and concludes that the whole thing is a scam and "BS."

Short of doing that, however, I think it's useful to deconstruct the concept of the "enlightened teacher" in hopes of becoming clearer about how such falls from grace happen, and what it implies for internal awareness and our argument as a whole.

Let's imagine a person who, through one method or another, achieves a profound spiritual experience akin (more or less) to enlightenment. If that person is under the guidance of a mature spiritual teacher, that teacher might make sure this student stays under wraps until ready to teach, assuring that the newbie guru doesn't besmirch the master's good name. Such a new teacher won't be a problem, as he or she is likely to be cautious when finally emerging and won't make such incredible claims. That kind of teacher, while having the potential downside of being doctrinaire, doesn't enter into our story much. He or she will be outnumbered in the spiritual marketplace by the much greater number who strike out on their own or always were on their own.

But let's imagine the case which happens more frequently, where the student and potential spiritual teacher has a profound experience *outside* the guidance of a benevolent and wise master. The newbie has an experience, the content of which is actually unimportant here, since we know it varies widely between individuals and have no way of assessing it. In addition to the experience they have, what is *more* important to our analysis is a memory of the experience, an interpretation of the experience, and an *expectation* of what that experience may mean for them in the future. In other words—a fantasy.

We have seen from our earlier exploration how important fantasy is in producing happiness, and we can imagine that a powerful and rare experience such as the newbie teacher had can provoke an equally powerful expectation of good things to come. Those things might include the expectation of more cosmic experiences, finding out the meaning of life, overcoming death, performing miracles or whatever. In other words, just as the act of purchasing a new self-help book or taking a workshop almost automatically produces a sensation of happiness out of the fantasy of an improved life, so would this experience do the same, and in spades. So in addition to whatever afterglow of the enlightenment experience the newbie guru has, there is a sense of happiness built into his thoughts after it.

Now add one more factor into the equation. I have discussed earlier in the chapter how interior awareness can reduce stress by creating distance. It seems likely that a powerful internal experience of spirituality also creates a greater distance from both external events and the emotions triggered by them. So what we have is a person with a profound experience, a fantasy of what that experience means, and a greater distance from his or her own emotions and circumstances—all making that person to appear content, even blissful.

If you are feeling not exactly comfortable with this person holding the destiny of others in his hands, you are not alone. Add into the equation the temptation of that person to exaggerate his or her experience to assure success in the spiritual marketplace, and you then have a bunch of people who are looking up to that newbie guru with a perhaps exaggerated sense of awe and adulation.

You may object that I myself have argued that happy people act better than unhappy people, so what is the problem with a happy guru? The problem is that while some of the teacher's happiness is based on the afterglow of their experience, a substantial amount is likely based on the fantasies they have newly constructed out of that experience. And since the other product of their experience is a greater emotional distance, the process of coming down to earth and integrating their experience is going to be delayed, but it is going to happen.

You may recall, from the earlier discussion of distance, the idea that there are both thick and thin-boundaried people. Let's take a look at what could happen if each of these kinds of people, as a spiritual teacher, "returns to earth" after having a profound spiritual experience.

Thin-boundaried people would experience the reintegration process comparatively rapidly. Once back down, they would have a choice to either a) go back to their practice and hope for more lasting results the next time, or b) continue to present themselves as a spiritual teacher but as a more modest one with a human side. Of course, we know that in the spiritual marketplace showing any human vulnerability is not a good choice in terms of gaining market share, so to speak, but it could work if one's goals are not too great.

On the other hand, thick-boundaried people will experience quite a different trajectory, taking more time before their "return to earth" because their natural emotional distance was already much greater. Because of that greater time span, they will have spent much more time as an "elevated" person and have gotten more used to thinking of themselves in those terms. Therefore, their self concept as being enlightened will be that much stronger.

In general, thick-boundaried people are less skilled in noticing and expressing their emotions than thin-boundaried ones, so it seems likely to me that when they start to feel the discomfort of disturbing emotions, they would be more likely to try to re-distance themselves. This might be done through meditating more, or perhaps, if that fails, with drugs or sex. In addition, because of their greater distance, any influence their emotions and drives would have on them would be unconscious to them, perhaps expressing through some kind of acting out through anger or manipulation to relieve the discomfort. It is in this tendency that, I believe, there is the greatest potential for the guru problems we end up reading or hearing about in the media.

You may also recall the distinction between pain and suffering. It seems likely that many would-be gurus fail to understand the difference and feel they must resist the pain or it would be evidence of unenlightenment. Yet we have seen before that pain is largely unavoidable and suffering too (at least to some degree) is difficult to eliminate. So when either appears it puts the would-be guru in a difficult position.

But there is one more factor that we need to consider. Because of the nature of the spiritual marketplace, it is bad advertising to have a guru with a drug or sex or anger or depression problem. The result, of course, is not that those problems decrease, but rather that they get acted out in secret. This is the reason for inner circles that surround spiritual teachers, as such a structure limits access to only those who are so committed, they can be trusted not to rat their teacher out. So on top of all the contradictions already described, we now have a situation where secrecy and hypocrisy are added to the equation. This scenario could go a long way in explaining the "downfall" of popular gurus over the past few decades, such as the Indian spiritual teacher Rajneesh, and more recently, the self-help guru and author James Ray, who kept people inside an Arizona sweat lodge too long, resulting in the death of two.

Remember that perhaps contrary to what you believe or have read, a spiritual experience does not wipe out the conceptual and/or emotional framework a person has spent a lifetime developing. The only change is that it has given them an afterglow, a difference in perspective, and greater emotional distance from their human side.

SPIRITUAL BY-PASSING

One final downside of seeking happiness through spirituality is a phenomenon known as "spiritual by-passing." Any person who has had some experience of adjusting their distance by interior awareness and also learned a little spiritual philosophy is potentially susceptible to the practice of spiritual bypassing. Essentially, this is simply recasting emotional issues into spiritual ones for the purpose of avoiding emotional discomfort, a practice that can be both dishonest and unhealthy. For example, if you don't get the job: *Wow, I guess it wasn't meant to be.* Or you get dumped: *Oh well, all things must pass.* It is common in society to avoid emotions, because emotions can be uncomfortable, and among spiritual or religious people that discomfort is even greater, because they literally hold themselves to a "higher" standard.

You may remember the religious admonitions against strong emotions that I quoted at the beginning of the Chapter 3 on emotions. These judgments are still held as valid by many groups of people, and indeed, such judgments are often cited as the actual *raison d'etre* for being spiritual or religious. However, as I proposed in that chapter, the best response is not emotional repression but the establishment of an appropriate distance from the emotions that neither represses them nor gets them swallowed up.

There is a reason for avoiding spiritual by-passing. If someone is using a belief to create distance from an emotion, that person is missing out on receiving life's lessons—which, you would think, would be the actual purpose of being on a path of spirituality or religion in the first place.

When I first meet spiritual seekers of one type or another, I sometimes ask them the question, *What have you learned in your life?* In a surprising number of cases, they answer with a platitude like, *Everything is One.* I then ask if that wasn't something they learned early on, and ask again, *Is there anything you have learned in the last ten years?* Again, I am often surprised at how difficult this question is to answer in a way that conveys any substance.

One would think that a seeker is a person who would be trying to gain wisdom every day, but that's often not what I find. Rather, it is as if in their search for ultimate meaning, they are like a robot vacuum cleaner, stuck in a corner and going endlessly over the same piece of carpet while leaving the rest of the room untouched. Of course, it is also possible that people I've asked have learned many things but think what they've learned isn't important since it isn't "spiritual." But along with bypassing emotions, they could also be bypassing life lessons!

In any case, you can see that the biggest problem with people who take up a path of seeking the truth, particularly those identified as spiritual teachers, can sometimes be the opposite from the everyday person's, due to spiritual by-passing and other pitfalls. That doesn't mean that connecting with a person who has had spiritual experiences is worthless—far from it. One can benefit from their perspective, their insight, their energy, and even their distance. But none of that negates any of the points of this book.

ARE WE DOING ANYTHING WRONG?

If you ask a spiritual teacher or read a spiritual book to answer the question, *Am I doing anything wrong?* The answer is undoubtedly *Yes*. Certainly, you are not doing anything right: You are not perfect, you are not peaceful, you get angry or irritated, you worry, you stress out, you are not selfless, you are not living in the present moment, you are not "happy for no reason." But you *will be*, you are promised, if you buy the book, take the seminar, join the cult, or whatever is being sold in that corner of the spiritual marketplace.

And so you buy the book, sign up for the seminar, or join the group, and you are given perhaps one or two useful tools, perhaps a kind of meditation, or an insight about one aspect of life, so you can finally "do it right." The rest is basically an attempt at thought suppression, which, as we've seen over and over in this book, tends ultimately to fail. Then, after repeated failures, you are likely to develop some negative beliefs about yourself, which the next teacher, book, or seminar can exploit and tell you is your *real* problem, and you can start all over again.

Sometimes you get lucky and a teacher has some real wisdom to offer. This happened for me when a few years ago, I was brought by a friend to a Buddhist temple on the island of Maui. He introduced me to the head monk, a young man of obvious intelligence and sensitivity who, after a long conversation that impressed me, invited me to sit in on the evening class. I happily agreed, but was disappointed to find the class was a long series of explanations of arcane Buddhist scriptures that were very taxing on my attention. Mercifully, that period ended and the monk asked for questions. A number of students asked convoluted questions that the monk fielded as best he could, but I had a sense the students weren't completely satisfied and maybe weren't even asking the questions that were really on their minds. I pondered over this for a while after the class ended.

Eventually, the monk made his way over to me and asked me what I thought of the class. I said that I found it difficult to understand some of the more complex Buddhist scriptures, but also that he might have misunderstood the underlying intention of his students' questions. He was intrigued and asked what I meant. I responded, "Well, I think what the students were really asking is how do they know if they are making progress on the spiritual path?"

"Oh yes," he smiled. "My older students often ask this question. I tell them if they are increasingly understanding the changeableness of life and increasingly accepting themselves as they are, then they are progressing."

I was stunned by the simplicity of his answer that many more prominent teachers had never given to this basic concern of spiritual students. Even though I had yet to go through my motel room experience in Carson City and the other experiences during the same period that changed my life, I knew what the monk was saying was the truth.

The problem, however, is that you can't just *tell* people to be that way—more self-accepting and detached. If you do, you are again attempting to use thought suppression of any opposite thoughts which will never work. Something else is needed, which I will reveal as I've promised in Chapter Seven of this book. But if you think about it, the monk's insights are exactly the ones I am trying to impart in this book, which are that life is ever-changing, causing our thoughts and moods to change, and, generally speaking, *we are not doing anything wrong!*

But we have set ourselves up for being sold a bill of goods. Again, not by doing anything wrong, but only by having a natural desire to be happier and lacking a full understanding of the complexity of the human mind.

CHAPTER 6

THE NEW AGE

When I go into a New Age bookstore today, I have a very different reaction than my earlier sense of wonder I mentioned in the last chapter. Wonder gave way to disillusionment, but now—as Elvis Costello once sang in his humorously titled song about Angels wanting to wear his red shoes -- that he used to be disgusted, but now tried to be amused.

Much of what is popular in the New Age spiritual marketplace these days are those ideas most often ridiculed: Angels, people in the center of the earth, extra-terrestrials, DNA activations, etc. Putting aside the issue of validity, we can see that the popularity of New Age beliefs is typically based on fantasy. Whether there *really* are Angels, ETs or people in the center of the earth, it's the fantasy that when these exotic things do show up, they will somehow solve all of our problems - rather than just sit there not doing anything for us.

Personally, I can't wait. I am going to get my DNA activated and my chakras healed right now, just to be ready! As I've said, the appeal of DNA activations and chakra healings is the expectation or fantasy that life will improve as soon as you get them—just like everything else you are urged to hang your hopes on. Even further, if you know your personal Angel, you can have the added expectation that he or she will help and protect you. It's not the truth of this *really* happening, but rather the fantasy and expectation of it happening, that makes us so happy, because we can generally never know whether they helped us or not.

In spite of all this, as I have mentioned, much of the popular culture has absorbed New Age spirituality in the same way as, in earlier eras, large swathes of Catholicism and the Protestant Ethic were absorbed into the respective cultures of their times. Just as those religious ideologies had profound implications for how people lived their lives, New Age "religion" has affected our culture and how we live in the modern world.

Let's see now how some specific and less exotic New Age concepts apply to the search for happiness in modern times. (If you are not interested in such pursuits, you are welcome at this point to skip ahead to the next chapter, but if you are, please come along with me.)

Nine New Age concepts I intend to examine for their relevance to happiness are:

1. Synchronicity
2. Interconnectedness
3. Perfectibility and the Law of Karma
4. Retrospective Determinism
5. Karma
6. Reincarnation
7. Inner Guidance
8. Creating Reality
9. Energy

1. SYNCHRONICITY

Synchronicity, as I have illustrated in the last chapter, is all about the way things work together. It was based on Jung's understanding of Eastern religion and his attempt to make sense of the oracular tradition which included the *I Ching*, an object of special interest to him. How could throwing yarrow stalks, the traditional method of the *I Ching*, possibly divine the future?

The argument that Jung offered for other sources of divination, such as Tarot cards, crystal balls, tea leaves or the ancient Roman method of reading entrails, is that the symbolic nature of an oracle allowed the diviner to look into his own unconscious via the archetypes of the symbols. This then would allow his mind to bring forth knowledge from what Jung called the *collective unconscious* or God. The Tarot deck contains pictorial symbols on its cards, and the "pictures" that appear in tea leaves or in a crystal ball can act as a kind of Rorschach test, allowing an attuned diviner to see not just the contents of his own unconscious but that of the collective unconscious.

But with the *I Ching*, it doesn't work that way. Although each hexagram is attached to an image, the meanings of them, though often obscure, are very specific. The *I Ching* itself has an unusual explanation for how it works. A divination from the *I Ching* is written by casting stalks or coins to arrive at each line of the hexagram, but the writing is done from the bottom to the top instead of the normal method of top down. The message is that time is standing on its head, moving into the future instead of moving into the past as events normally do. This is an intriguing idea, but the *I Ching's* message probably just seemed odd to Jung. Instead of noting it as significant, Jung went back to the more essential view of synchronicity, which is that everything is part of the whole, so why couldn't everything be interconnected?

The importance of synchronicity for us is that it offers an additional hope for our potential happiness in the future, in that it implies a universal harmony that can be tapped into—if you can relax enough to get in touch with it. In other words, there is a flow that you can indeed go with if you can let go of all the trying, and that flow can help you better achieve what Epictetus advised—not wasting your time on things that can't be changed. By showing us where we are in the cycle of change and counseling us to restrain in most instances, the *I Ching* is giving us a boost in the very area which is most difficult—knowing when to change something.

So despite being "undermined" in our quest from below by the unconscious, we are potentially being aided from above by the spiritual realm. But are there other ideas out there in the New Age frontier that would be of benefit? Let's take a look through the rest of the New Age concepts and debate them for down sides and possible benefits.

2. INTERCONNECTEDNESS

Viewed in different ways by different people, the notion of *interconnectedness* can be seen in three different perspectives: The first perspective is based on *non-dualism*, sometimes called "monism," which says that the difference between all things in existence is essentially illusory and that there is only one thing in existence, which is God. A second view is that everything is energetically interconnected by an underlying spiritual or "energy" field. The third view is that we are all part of a complex, living eco-system that has been described by environmentalist James Lovelock as the "Gaia hypothesis."

The first perspective, non-dualism, is the one most common in New Age thought, but that is unfortunate, because I believe Jung would have been uncomfortable with it. After all, he chose the concept of *individuation* as the goal of life, a concept which is a polar opposite to the *nirvana* of Buddhism. Nirvana, literally translated, means "snuffing out," as in extinguishing, emphasizing that nothing truly exists, not even God. To Jung and others, the concept of nirvana deprived life of ultimate meaning, since the goal is only to stop existing, or be "snuffed out."

However, many Buddhists, even though they still embrace the concept of nirvana, use a better term, *interconnectedness*. Or, as the Vietnamese Buddhist monk Thich Nat Hanh says, *inter-being*. The real value of these terms in Buddhist practice and New Age thought is to highlight the common interest of all people, and indeed all beings, in pursuit of a more harmonious existence. We are all one humanity, the thinking goes, so to make war is ridiculous. We are all *inter-being* with nature, so let us live in harmony with our environment.

In any case, the non-dualistic notion of oneness is not one that penetrates far into the mainstream. Most people feel far more comfortable with the notion of God as a personal or impersonal force that interpenetrates all beings than with a notion that "God is real, but we aren't." The idea of "the Force" in the *Stars Wars* movies may be a good illustration of the former, and it is one that, in my experience, even many atheists are comfortable with. It is also *simpatico* with traditional religion to a certain extent. Christ's statement, "The Kingdom of God is within," is more compatible with an inter-penetrating spiritual field than it is with a Father in Heaven who exists somewhere up there in the sky.

I think the reason for the new popularity of non-dualism expressed as interconnectedness relates indirectly to happiness. There is a long literature in the West about alienation. In our modern, fast-paced and impersonal society, we are often far in both physical and emotional distance from family and real community. Interconnectedness helps us feel connected to humanity and the environment in a way that is no longer typically possible in a modern society.

I would probably be remiss in not addressing the pathological side of non-dualism, which may well also account for its popularity. This is that non-dualism is also useful in spiritually by-passing emotions. I have a friend who, whenever problems arise, says, "Well, I don't really exist, so there is no problem. It's all an illusion anyway." I think most of us would find that cold comfort, not to mention a little odd. So here my vote is for interconnectedness, but not necessarily for a "oneness" that denies individual existence.

3. PERFECTIBILITY AND THE LAW OF ATTRACTION

Perfectibility assumes that human beings are potentially unlimited and any fault can be corrected. The lack of success in any area of life only means there is room for future improvement.

Such an optimistic view stands in contrast to traditional religious notions that human life is inherently sinful, ignorant or limited, and that suffering is inevitable or necessary. The reason for suffering in the more New Age view is not sinful nature or God's punishment, or even inscrutable will, but because lessons must be learned in life for the maturation of the soul. This process is a life-long one, and indeed, if one believes in reincarnation, not limited to a single life.

The benefit of perfectibility for happiness should be obvious. Any fault can be corrected, and it is indeed our destiny to overcome all faults and become "perfect" sooner or later. The question of *What's wrong with me?* needn't be so troublesome or depressing with such a view.

One aspect of perfectibility is the much quoted Law of Attraction, often invoked by self-help books for aiding people in their attempts to have successful careers, relationships, and other endeavors. (It is also is a popular method for "creating reality," a topic I will discuss later in this chapter.) The Law of Attraction is simple: Like attracts like. The energy put out by your thoughts, emotions, and unconscious patterns attract people and events into your life. In books like the popular 2005 bestseller *The Secret* and dozens of others going back a hundred years, the idea is promoted that you can create success by visualizing it and having more positive thoughts.

In recent years, the field of physics known as *quantum mechanics* has been cited as the operating principle behind this approach, but previously it was explained by a *cybernetic* principle, first in the book *Psycho-Cybernetics*, by Malcolm Maltz. I will note that while the standard interpretation of quantum theory states that observation of a particle influences it (the Schrodinger's Cat paradox), there is nothing in the theory that says it can be applied deliberately or on a larger scale than the sub-atomic. Nevertheless, even without intentionality, the Law of Attraction is still potentially operative in a more neutral way. The principle of synchronicity could be operated by the Law of Attraction, in that the natural flow of interconnectedness could be what causes people and events to gravitate together.

The Secret is based on the notion that you can visualize your goals and bring them into existence. That book has been much criticized for numerous reasons, including that it deflects people away from concrete actions and redirects them to mental ones, that it promotes magical thinking rather than resourcefulness, and that it blames people for their thinking when adversity occurs.

Nevertheless, I had to try it for myself and discover my own results. One amusing anecdote I can tell about my largely unsuccessful experiments with visualization is a thought experiment I performed questioning one of its supporting arguments. The premise is, as given in several sources I've read, that visualization works because everything you can imagine must exist somewhere in the universe—if you can imagine it, it exists. Therefore, all you need to do is magnetize whatever it is you want to you. Leaving the physics of that aside, the thought struck me as strange. Having read Doug Adam's novel *Hitchhikers Guide to the Galaxy*, I immediately thought of the planet of "intelligent mattresses" described in that whimsical novel. It hardly seemed likely that such things could exist, even given the vast number of stars in the universe, but that improbability didn't necessarily constitute a proof against it. I resolved to come up with one that did.

I reasoned that there certainly must be something that I could imagine that was logically impossible in all circumstances. This is what I came up with: Imagine a machine that was immediately receptive to all thoughts in the universe, and the minute it was thought of, that machine destroyed the universe! I confess that I had a moment of hesitation before completing the thought, but in the interest of science, I proceeded. The fact that you are reading this now is proof that no such machine exists anywhere in the universe, and therefore the argument is false!

Of course, visualization could work without that argument, but after years of watching my acquaintances fail more times than succeed, I would probably rewrite the Law of Attraction. I believe that the Law of Attraction is constantly bringing things into our lives, if at all, by magnetizing our unconscious thoughts rather than our conscious ones. When our conscious thoughts are consistent with our unconscious thoughts, only then can our conscious thoughts magnetize events or things to us.

Just how difficult it is to attract something from the conscious mind is illustrated by a story a friend recently told me. A mutual acquaintance had become a workshop leader and was teaching people to "manifest" their desires. As part of her instruction, the leader told the participants they should visualize what they wanted down to the last detail. One of the participants asked her if she was currently trying to manifest anything. She answered that she was trying to create a relationship. When asked how long she was trying, her response was 20 years. Well, at least she was honest, right?

Therefore, I would also like to hypothesize an opposite but complementary law: The Law of Repulsion, which could possibly explain the workshop leader's long ordeal to manifest a relationship. This law is based on the principle that if you are attached to the idea of something that you want (e.g. a relationship), you push it away from you. From a psychological perspective, you can see why this would happen. If a person is overly attached to some goal, they would become anxious about achieving it. The anxiety could cause them to not think clearly about opportunities, perhaps miss an opportunity while worrying about it, or even worse, blow an opportunity to obtain their goal due to nervousness. (I will explain more about why this occurs when I discuss Viktor Frankl's concept of *paradoxical intention* in the next chapter.) From a spiritual perspective, such anxiety would produce an energetic reaction that instead of magnetizing something to a person, would create an opposite dynamic, i.e. repulsion, and push it further away.

As you might have noticed, my view of the Law of Attraction is much more ambivalent than the standard one. While the Law of Attraction does explain why synchronicity isn't always bringing happiness and good things into one's life—because you attract from your unconscious mind—it is a double-edged sword. As I've said, it can be just one more thing to blame yourself over, and additionally, it doesn't seem to ever be able to be proven wrong to its followers. If the Law of Attraction isn't working, the thinking goes, then you just need to try harder. I think in the end, the intentional practice of the Law Attraction is more trouble than it is worth for our happiness; however, it can be useful if you see it as a clue to understanding why you are attracting unwanted things, and if you are willing to include the unconscious in the equation.

To their credit, most New Agers who take up the practice of the Law of Attraction are aware of the unconscious mind and the obstacles that it presents. Their solution, however, is to try to program the *sub*conscious with affirmations, repeating positive statements with the intention of changing how they think of themselves and others. In my view, this can only produce limited success. The reason is the existence of the deep unconscious that I mentioned in Chapter 5. To the degree that one can program the subconscious at all, it seems unlikely that programming will go all the way into the deep unconscious mind.

One final critique: Even if the Law of Attraction works, it essentially solves nothing. Say you could attract everything you wanted. You would be happy for a minute, but then, as I've said before, *the game goes on*. You would be in exactly the position of every super rich person, which is always wanting more. And while money can avoid some sources of unhappiness, it doesn't buy happiness at all. In fact, as I mentioned earlier, according to a Princeton University study, there is no evidence that having any more money than $70,000 (2010 dollars) has any effect on a person's happiness at all.

In fact, I am reminded of a Twilight Zone episode I saw on TV many years ago. After his death, a man wakes up in the afterlife, surrounded by beautiful women and sunny skies. He walks into stores to find everything is free for the asking. He goes into a casino, and every bet he makes wins. He enjoys his perfect life for a little while, but gradually it gets annoying. Finally, he gets depressed and asks to talk to whoever is in charge. Eventually, he finds a "supervisor" and says to him, "Look, man... I'm bored. Just send me to the 'other place.'" The supervisor laughs and says, "This *is* the 'other place.'"

Finally, the role of adversity in life can't be avoided, for as we all know, many of life's lessons come not from our successes but from our failures.

4. RETROSPECTIVE DETERMINISM

Another popular concept is what I call *retrospective determinism*, which means that everything that happened *had* to happen. Most people evoke this when a valued goal or outcome doesn't work out, saying, *Oh, I guess it wasn't meant to be*. But it can also be about the things that *were* meant to be, in which case you would say, *I guess it was meant to be*. If you look back through your life, it is easy to see in retrospect how you made the decisions you did, even if they were mistakes in the end. It is also impossible to disprove a certain amount of fate happening in life when you look at things that way.

If true, this determinism could occur through karma, which is the current effects of a person's past deeds, or it could occur by the process of the unconscious mind working itself out, as detailed just above. My own notion is this: just as a submerged body tends to float to the surface, things repressed into the unconscious want to resurface. It takes energy to keep things repressed, and the friction between people's life events and their personalities tends to bring those things out. This dynamic happens in personal relationships over time, and it happens to a lesser degree in less intimate settings as well. So the idea of determinism is essentially an optimistic one—that repressed, unsolved problems tend to surface in the hope of being ultimately resolved. The compatibility between karma and the psychological explanation here should be obvious, in that both karma and repressed issues have a tendency to "bubble up" to the surface.

Finally, if we are all different bundles of psychological conditioning, and if our thoughts are simply echoes of our impulses, as Wegner controversially suggests in his later book, *The Illusion of Conscious Will,* then we can certainly go along with determinism to at least some degree. In any case, I am sympathetic to this determinism, because it fits well with what Epictetus has to say. The past is one thing you cannot change. The only thing you can change is your viewpoint on the past. Regretting past mistakes generally only helps your life if it produces a resolve to learn from those mistakes and avoid them next time.

5. KARMA

Karma is a term that has made its way into the popular culture in a significant manner over the last 40 years. As you probably know, the basic notion is similar to the popular saying, *What goes around, comes around,* or the Biblical phrase, *As ye sow, so shall ye reap.* In other words, karma is payback for bad deeds, a kind of rebalancing of the record.

However, it strikes me that this more conventional notion is not the only explanation of karma. Ultimately, karma relies on reincarnation to explain current harsh circumstances. A person born into poverty, war, or a personal handicap may be balancing bad deeds done in a past lifetime. But it could also be the case that a dynamic of lack of self-worth could explain one's birth into harsh circumstances, just as much as any bad deeds done previously.

Just as the lesson a woman in an abusive relationship must learn is that she deserves better, the lesson of a person born into poverty could be that they, too, deserve better. The actions such a person might take to get out of poverty would then be consistent with learning that lesson. This explanation seems better than the traditional notion of karma, that you should accept your fate with the hope of being promoted in a later life. How ironic it would be if the very teaching of traditional karma turned out to be the thing that kept a person bound to their circumstances.

The New Age version that we get what we think we deserve based on our self-worth, is clearly more humane. It is interesting to compare the traditional notion of karma with the newer one in regards to wealthy people. In the traditional view, people are wealthy because of their past good deeds, while in the new view, it is simply because they have higher self esteem. The bad behavior of the wealthy in the current era certainly leads me, for one, to favor the newer explanation—you get what you believe you deserve— over the more traditional one of karma—that wealthy people have good karma from past lives.

So which version is true? We can't know that, but it seems reasonable to assume that both may be going on in different circumstances, if indeed reincarnation is true. So here I am going to be neutral, and you can pick and choose.

6. REINCARNATION

I mentioned earlier that belief in an afterlife could be very helpful for experiencing happiness in old age. But it is difficult and odd to *try* to believe something, just because it is a good idea to believe it, as Voltaire's critique of *Pascal's Wager* has demonstrated—that even though it is a safer bet to believe in God than not, it doesn't make it any easier to change your mind if you don't believe.

The best we can do, since we can't know for sure about an afterlife, is to examine the alternatives. There are three: 1) when you are dead you are dead, 2) reincarnation, and 3) heaven or hell.

Let's look at the first one, which is that when you die, all existence ceases. While it is not possible to prove the continued existence of the soul, there is one consideration that can be made. In the physical universe, there is a law of conservation of matter and energy—nothing can ever be lost. Although one can be transmuted into the other, the stability of the system is maintained through this principle. It would be consistent with this principle if life were to continue in a different form after death, conserving the energy of consciousness, albeit in a transmuted form.

Regarding the next two, and comparing heaven vs. reincarnation, there are a couple of points that lean toward reincarnation, if it comes down to a choice. First, it seems somewhat absurd that a soul would incarnate once and then after death, journey to heaven or hell to spend billions of years. With the current estimate of 80 billion people who have lived on earth, heaven and hell would have to keep getting larger and larger. Furthermore, with the possibility of life on other planets from some 300 billion stars in this galaxy and some 400 billion galaxies in the universe, the size of heaven and hell would have to be enormous—and to what end?

Another problem, somewhat more humorous, is the problem of animals. Allegedly, dogs do not have souls, but try telling that to pet owners. The loyalty of a dog is often far superior to that of any human. I, for one, would have a hard time arguing against letting dogs into heaven. And if you admit dogs, what about rabbits? They seem so sweet and innocent... So, you see, there is a problem.

On the other hand, reincarnation could be a comparatively economical solution. Souls could reincarnate innumerable times, thereby reducing the exponentially enormous numbers, and then even animals could be included in the process.

All kidding aside, there is actually some evidence for reincarnation. The investigations of psychiatrist Ian Stevenson in his *Children Who Remember Past Lives* found a prototypical pattern for his subjects, starting when a small child is two to four years of age. The child usually began by talking to his parents or siblings of a life he led in another but nearby time and place. The child felt a considerable pull back toward the events of the life and frequently insisted that his parents let him return to the place where he (supposedly) lived formerly. If the child made enough specific statements about his previous life, the parents reluctantly would begin inquiries about their accuracy. Eventually, if indeed accurate, members of the two families would meet and ask the child whether he recognized any part of his supposed previous existence.

Stevenson created a network of volunteers to find these cases of spontaneous past life recall. He then questioned both the family of the living child and the "prior" one, while attempting to ensure that they had no contact and that no information was exchanged. After trying to obtain detailed information about the deceased, hopefully including information not known to anyone else, he would try to verify that the child actually did know this hidden information.

The publication of Stevenson's book was delayed when it was discovered that one of his interpreters in India had been accused of dishonesty. Stevenson returned with different interpreters, and this time asked even more detailed questions. He still concluded that reincarnation was the "best possible explanation" after reviewing the new evidence.

Returning to the original question, we must finally ask: *Considering that both heaven and reincarnation may have been the product of a revelation, is there any way in which they can be reconciled?*

Looking for reconciliation is a wise practice whenever comparing differing paradigms, whether philosophical or scientific. To my mind, it is possible that the reincarnation paradigm could actually contain the heaven/hell one, in the same way that Einsteinian physics includes, contains, and surpasses Newtonian physics. It is possible that the soul goes through a heaven or hell experience upon dying, as the person leaves the physical reality, entering a reality made up solely of his or her feelings. This is similar to what is described in the *Tibetan Book of the Dead*, as one goes through the *bardo* states between lives. But a few moments of complete ecstasy or horror could seem, after death, like an eternity, and the notion of heaven and hell occur simply as an incomplete vision of the after death experience, rather than a false one.

As you can see my vote is for reincarnation, but you may disagree.

7. INNER GUIDANCE

One of the more intriguing aspects of New Age philosophy is that of *inner guidance*. Here the notion is that you can follow an easier course through life by listening to the "still, small voice within," and paying attention to the vibration or energies of different things or choices. You can learn to tune into that voice, your inner guidance, through practice and letting go, developing what can be observed as intuition or "psychic sensing."

Pete Sander's book, *You Are Psychic,* lists four ways of tuning into your psychic senses, and thus your inner guidance, and suggests that each person differs in terms of which senses are easiest and most practical for them. He states that people are either visionary, auditor, feeling or knowing. The visionary person "sees" things about events or situations, perhaps a red or green light when they close their eyes while thinking of a choice. An auditory person will hear a voice telling them information, and a feeling person will get a gut feeling about what is appropriate to do. Finally, a knowing person will just "know" what is right or what is going to happen. Sanders ascribes these different points of access to different parts of the body, and assesses the strengths and weaknesses of each approach. Again, his view is everyone has the ability, but most need some training to discover and develop their strongest sense(s).

One of the side benefits of this "psychic" sensing is the potential ability to resolve the serenity prayer dilemma—knowing what to change and what not to change. Sometimes it may be easier to just sense the answer or to see or hear it, than to puzzle it out.

Underlying this perspective of inner guidance are parts of the philosophy mentioned earlier, including the notions of perfectibility and the potential goodness of life, that we can avoid at least some suffering by paying attention to the clues offered through our intuitive side. But inner guidance is also somewhat paradoxical to the notion of retrospective determinism, which states that whatever happens, is what was supposed to happen and not a mistake. Where was that small inner voice when you needed it? If you'd listened to it, you may not have needed retrospective determinism to explain events that were or weren't supposed to happen.

Sometimes the benefit that results from making a "mistake" is so great, it may actually be guided. A friend once complained to me how he'd often be "guided" to enter into relationships with women that then turned out to be volatile rather than peaceful. Someone had finally suggested to him that perhaps the purpose of the guidance was not to avoid issues but to have him confront issues by putting him in situations that would force him to grow. Of course, another possibility is that he interpreted the guidance he received incorrectly and went for the wrong women, but let's give him the benefit of the doubt!

In any case, you can see that the model of guidance is one that can be applied with varying degrees of sophistication. Obviously, many people assume that a thought or a sign of some sort means they are supposed to go off in a particular direction, and it leads nowhere in particular. Then the individual can rationalize the experience by essentially making up some significance where there is none. I am reminded of a famous UCLA experiment by Harold Garfinkle from the 1960s. He advertised that students could get a free telephone session with a psychologist as long as they asked only yes or no questions. In fact, the call was made to the experimenter, who simply answered randomly based on flipping a coin. You might think that most people did not find such random answers useful, but a full three-quarters of the students said they did.

To understand how Garfinkle's subjects could make meaning of nothing, you need to imagine how an interview might go. Here's a scenario:

Q: I've told you about the situation between me and my father, so my question now is, who is to blame? Is it me?
A: [flips coin]: No.
Q: Okay, then it *is* my father, right?
A: [flips coin]: No.
Q: Oh, so you are saying it is both of our faults?
A: [flips coin]: No.
Q: Huh? Oh, you mean it's neither of our faults?
A: [flips coin]: No.
Q: [totally puzzled now]. I don't understand. [Thinks some more]. Well, then do you mean it is actually my mom who is creating the situation?
A: [flips coin]: Yes.
Q: [pleased]. Aha. That is very perceptive. I never would have thought of that.
Thank you so much!

I am sure that everyone who has ever read an astrology column or watched TV psychic John Edward has suspected that some kind of silliness like this is going on, where people are trying to fit reality into some odd box. But the truth is, this is somewhat inevitable. In fact, many dream researchers claim that dreams are simply random firings of neurons and all meanings are imposed from outside. Yet anyone who has read Freud's *Interpretation of Dreams* cannot help but think there is something to dreams. I personally have interpreted dozens, if not hundreds of dreams by various people often with profound results.

There are a few rejoinders to the critique of randomness: First, that randomness does not negate every possibility of causation—there may be complex variables or patterns yet unfound that when discovered reduce or eliminate the apparent randomness. Second, if life is random, then stupid people should succeed as much as smart people, and despite the occasional exception, that is not the case. Finally, while there are many things that happen in life that may be random, there are many other things that are the direct result of our actions and decisions—even though we cannot be sure of their outcomes

So in spite of all the difficulties, no one would advise you, *Don't try to learn from life.* There do seem to be patterns we can grasp accurately for help, but we are always risking when we are connecting the dots. In essence, the existentialists are right: as individuals we are in the business of making meaning. Our only criteria should be *how well it is working.*

For inner guidance to be successful, you must able to hear or sense that guidance and then actually attempt to follow it. You've probably had the experience where you were about to do something but suddenly had a gut feeling that it wasn't going to work out the way you wanted. If you stubbornly went ahead, you probably found out that your attachment to the particular choice blinded you to something you should have paid attention to. Carl Jung used the term *preconscious cognition* to explain such occurrences. You perceived it on some level, but your cognitive structures, your belief system did not let the idea filter in. Nevertheless, the intuitive or emotional side of your personality was reacting.

Probably the most common situations in which this happens are romantic relationships. The "halo effect"—where one single favorable quality of a person is assumed to be more universal—can cause you to misjudge another as better than they actually are. But somehow, you may still have a bad feeling or nagging insecurity stemming from an unacknowledged perception of the reality. You may even try to bring up your concern, only to have it shot down and invalidated. Only in retrospect can you see the truth, which your gut feeling was telling you all along.

Guidance can also encourage you to take a risk you might not have taken if you were limited to your rational mind. That, of course, is a double-edged sword, but in many cases, it could open doors that might otherwise have been left closed.

All in all, I think guidance is probably quite useful, so long as it is tempered with common sense and reason.

8. CREATING REALITY

We have already discussed the way in which we create our reality—that is, how we create our interpretation or meaning of reality. But the New Age sense in which this occurs is even more radical.

Creating reality is simply - as in the theory behind visualization - that we are literally out-picturing reality from within our minds, from within our own belief systems. Reality in these terms becomes more fluid and almost like a dream. Just as every dream event reveals hints about the dreamer, its author, every life event may do as well, if reality is thus a result of one's belief system alone. At its worst, this view promotes a sense of limitlessness, that anything is possible, which may be out of touch with the greater reality.

I have friends or acquaintances who are creating perfect relationships, multi-millions of dollars and even physical immortality but only in their minds. In life, they have none of that. The proof, of course, will be in the pudding, but it is likely that at least some of them will never admit their failure, even despite its obviousness to others.

But in addition to the way in which we create the meaning of our reality, there is also a narrower way in which that meaning is certainly correct. It is well-known that an optimistic outlook tends to produce better results than a pessimistic one, if for no other reason than a pessimistic attitude has you give up earlier rather than persist until success. In that sense, you are always creating or destroying opportunities that might surface when circumstances change or new ideas come to mind.

Additionally, the idea of synchronicity also supports some notion of creative reality. If everything is all working together as synchronicity implies, the question is who is making it all work together? One answer might be God. But this makes God a very busy bee indeed, even busier than the traditional Prime Mover who only has to intervene in key moments in life.

But if every soul is creating its own reality, then the only question is how do all those realities harmonize? This is an important question, because in every relationship more than one person is creating the reality. The answer may be that there are agreements between the souls to either facilitate each other's creation or to move away. People would attract others who subconsciously wish to play out the complementary roles to their own.

On the subject of creating reality, I have a mixed opinion—I think the notion of creating one's reality can encourage us to take more responsibility for things that seem out of our control but have a mysterious way of showing up in our world - that is what we attract unconsciously. Anyone who has followed the romantic lives of their single friends notices how their friend can go into a room and meet a stranger, and that stranger fits exactly into the partnering pattern the single person has followed their entire life.

There's something more going on here, it would appear, than just anticipatory responses. We magnetize people into our lives that replicate our patterns, so the guy or girl you randomly meet at a party ends up behaving similarly to everyone else before. If you respond to that behavior unconsciously, you conclude, "all men are jerks" or "all women are teases." Or any of the thousand generalizations you might hear at the bar or at the gym. If you take responsibility for what you are attracting, you see it is a result of this unconscious magnetization.

On the other hand, "taking responsibility for creating one's reality" can be a good philosophy for justifying the rich and powerful, and blaming society's victims. And then there is *this*—reporter Ron Suskind quoting an aide on why an invasion of Iraq by U.S. forces was going to succeed:

> ...*The aide said that guys like me {Suskind} were "in what we call the reality-based community," which he defined as people who "believe that solutions emerge from a judicious study of discernible reality."* ...

"That's not the way the world really works anymore," the aide continued. "We're an empire now, and when we act, we create our own reality..."

The aide was allegedly the infamous Karl Rove. Apparently, though, reality decided to fight back and cause a quagmire, not a victory!

9. ENERGY

One of the most well-known aspects of New Age thinking is the concept of *energy* and especially what is referred to as the *coherent field of energy*.

According to many, everything is constantly emitting and receiving energy. Crystals, power vortexes, and energy healings all involve this principle, yet were almost unheard of a generation ago; now most people have at least a passing knowledge of them.

Some of it makes sense. If we think of the brain and body as a bio-energetic organism, it is not hard to see how that organism might send and receive energy. Body cells can work in the same way as battery cells giving off small amounts of electro-magnetic current. You may recall that Mesmer's first experiments utilized magnets to induce a "healing crisis." His term, *animal magnetism* reflects his opinion about the source of the phenomenon he discovered. Mesmer would probably be right at home with modern products like magnetic therapy bands and beds. A 2006 article by William Wells in the *Journal of Cell Biology* confirmed that wounds have electrical fields and that a small electrical current causes cells to migrate more quickly into the wound area to facilitate healing. Hopefully, Mesmer has reincarnated in time to be able to appreciate the validation of some of his theory!

Plants, too, are known to emit electromagnetic force. But what about rocks and crystals? Probably the best evidence for crystals is the crystal radio that some of the older readers might remember from their childhood. These unpowered radios were able to pick up radio signals with the aid of an antenna and earphone. But what about rocks and power vortexes? Here we will have to leave science and simply hypothesize that rocks may have sufficient quartz to have some small amount of force. Formations of land may somehow, by their shape or geography, tend to accumulate energy as well, creating power vortexes of the like reported in Sedona, Arizona, and other places around the world.

All this is well and good and perhaps useful for healing and/or meditation, but an even more interesting aspect to energy I would like to discuss is something called a *coherent field of energy*.

You probably know how magnets work and have seen pictures of a magnet placed into a suspension of iron particles. What happens is that the iron particles move out of their random placement into an alignment around the poles of the magnet. Likewise, if you look at the structure of a crystal under a microscope, there is an order and pattern of alignment that is dissimilar from other forms of rock.

What if I were to tell you that there is a place where energy, positive thinking, and Buddhism meet, in a certain kind of alignment that is called a "sweet spot?"

According to the Wikipedia, "a sweet spot is a place where a combination of factors results in a maximum response for a given amount of effort. In tennis, baseball, or cricket, a given swing will result in a more powerful hit if the ball strikes the racquet or bat on the latter's sweet spot." In acoustics, the sweet spot is the focal point between two speakers, where a person can hear the stereo audio mix the way it was intended to be heard by the mixer. When using surround-sound, this is the focal point between four or more speakers.

In terms of energy, I believe that a sweet spot occurs when a person's thinking is 100% aligned—without doubt, unconscious contradiction, or second thoughts. That is what I call a *coherent field of energy*. The thoughts we normally think interfere with each other constantly, simply from the random chatter our minds endlessly engage in and especially from the "noise" of unconscious sabotage and ironic processes. When aligned, the mental coherent field is a lot like the audiophile definition of a sweet spot, where there are no interfering waves to distort the signal, and a bit like the sports sweet spot, where a minimum of input has the maximum results.

Regarding positive thinking, a coherent field occurs when a person is 100% believing in what they are trying to manifest, without any conscious or subconscious resistance. If conscious manifestation works, it is clearly under those circumstances of a coherent field of energy.

Likewise, detachment from the Buddhist perspective works only when you fully let go of whatever object you want. Otherwise, you are only "trying" to be detached, not be truly detached. And that can be a painful situation, because you end up still attached to the original object and also attached to trying to let go, basically getting torn between the two.

On the other hand, when you actually completely let go of something, an odd kind of miracle can occur, which is that the thing you were worrying about losing comes back to you. It is as if the Law of Repulsion suddenly is neutralized, as it should be when there is nothing to resist. There is an old saying from the '60s, taken from the writings of Kahlil Gibran, that wisely advises, "If you love someone, let them go..." And I think most of us have had some experience of that particular dynamic working when we do let go.

Both of these—pure positive thinking (also known as faith) and detachment (letting go)—are examples of what can happen when the mind creates a coherent field. Keep this concept of a coherent field of energy in your mind as we continue through the remaining chapters to finish our exploration.

In a more general inquiry, we might ask, *How important is the concept of energy overall in human consciousness?* As with most things, probably less than its advocates hope and more than the skeptics believe. I met one energy healer who was convinced anything could be healed by energy healings if she could move the energy out of the person's body. I remarked that if her subject had a psychological complex, it seemed likely he or she would just recreate the original energy pattern even if the energy was removed. Still, healing modalities like acupuncture, Reiki and crystals seem to have some therapeutic effect, especially if combined with other appropriate methods.

SUMMING IT UP

So how much has the New Age paradigm contributed to the quest for fulfillment? The promotion of meditation for interior awareness, as mentioned in the previous chapter, is a clear plus. The New Age doctrines are a bit of a mixed bag, but at least arguably superior to the belief systems in conventional religions. To a large degree, especially when you include meditation and other aspects of interior awareness, they have replaced fear and guilt-based systems in those religions with an optimistic world-view. However, the focus on attracting and manifesting, despite its obvious appeal for producing happiness by fulfilling desires, remains a double-edged sword. It does seem likely that some form of this paradigm is usable, perhaps when combined with the psychological one.

Tht is certainly what I thought for many years, but unfortunately it appears there is *yet another* missing link in the quest for happiness, which is my subject in the next chapter.

CHAPTER 7

THE MEANING OF LIFE

In late September 1942, Viktor Frankl stood at a railway station in Germany. After being torn from the arms of his wife, whom he had recently married, he was on his way to a forced labor camp. He stared glumly at the long line of forlorn people on the railway platform under the grey skies, each clutching the few possessions they were allowed to carry. A German officer, whom he later found out to be the notorious Josef Mengele, was barking orders. As each man passed, the officer pointed them to a line either to the right or left, where different trains of cattle cars awaited the prisoners. He was sent to the left line. Noticing that his few friends were in the other line, he secretly switched while the officer was looking away. That random decision saved his life; the other line was sent straight to execution, while he and his friends were sent to the labor camp at Theresienstadt.

Frankl, a doctor, found work in the camp as a general practitioner in the prison clinic, even though there as virtually no medicine, trying to ease the hardships of the prisoners. His skills as a therapist were eventually noticed, and he was asked to help newcomers deal with their shock and grief, and prevent suicide while still performing the full daily duties of his labor detail. He was occasionally asked to give talks to his fellow prisoners to maintain their morale. In order to do this and bolster his own spirits, he would practice by giving imaginary talks on the "therapeutic experience" in prison camps. He observed that those who were most likely to survive were those who found some meaning in their dismal life.

That meaning for him was most severely tested when the treasured manuscript that he'd brought with him hoping to complete it was found by guards and destroyed. He resolved to write it over and eventually did, but the book that made him famous was the one he wrote after the war, entitled *Man's Search for Meaning*, about his experiences in the camp. He later published his rewritten first book as *The Doctor and the Soul*.

THE IMPORTANCE OF MEANING

It almost seems quaint in the current era to think of a "search for meaning." Nowadays, such a search might be considered indulgent when the choices for finding meaning in life are so plentiful. You can choose either a specific religion like Buddhism, Christianity, Islam, or beliefs like atheism or New Age. Or simply embrace materialism and pursue pleasure. Why try to blaze your own path when there are already so many well-trod roads?

But even in today's world, meanings are important. You saw in the last chapter, in a humorous way, how making meaning out of our experience is something we humans do, even in random situations, like the experiment with the fake therapist who flipped coins for answers. Fundamentally, the human capacity for meaning creation is essentially what makes us different from other forms of life.

In addition, the meanings we make are often the source of the values we hold. In my own studies in graduate school, I had already learned that larger meanings were often crucial to the determination of individual and social values, which was the reason I switched from the sociology of knowledge to the sociology of religion. Social scientists have long held that values create attitudes, and attitudes affect behaviors. So meanings are in essence the foundation of all human endeavor.

There's another way in which meanings are important. I have mentioned how we don't react directly to events and people, but rather we react to what we perceive those to be, and not the true reality. But even that is not the whole story. For example, if you see a rope in the dark, but perceive it as a snake, you will probably react in fear. But it is not the only reaction you might have. If you had never heard of snakes, your reaction will be different than if you had. Even if you knew it to be poisonous, you would likely react differently if you were feeling suicidal than if you were not. (*Go ahead, bite me! I don't want to live any more!*) How you react is determined by the meaning that you attach to your perception. So in a fundamental way, it can be said that you neither respond to reality, nor even to your perception of reality, but rather you are responding to *the meaning you ascribe to your perception of reality.*

For Frankl, to say that there was a single meaning in life was like asking, in his words, "What is the best move in chess?" That is because there are so many situations in which one might find oneself. As an existentialist, he believed that all meanings were constructed by the individual and that meaning in life differed for each person, and at different times in a person's life. He felt in general that meaning could be derived from three things: 1) devotion to a person or a higher cause, 2) confronting or meeting an event or person, or 3) a response to suffering.

For different people, the meaning might variously be a spiritual search, the challenge of following a particular religion, the love of a spouse or children, helping other people, changing the world, overcoming an addiction, or just making it through the day. People can even have more than one of these.

In the Nazi concentration camp, the challenge for prisoners was the suffering endured by being detained and forced to labor in horrifying conditions. In that situation, a person's response to despair and hopelessness was critical for survival. Frankl saw how men walked right up to the camp's electrified fence to die when they gave up hope, and how the death rate spiked immediately after holidays when the illusory hope of being freed by an arbitrary date was dashed. Survival then depended on a realistic view that saw circumstances exactly as they were rather than as false hope that would be disappointed.

Interestingly, this insight of Frankl's was the same one shared by Admiral James Stockdale in the book *Good to Great* by James Collins. Stockdale, who you may remember as a latter-day follower of Epictetus, said when asked by Collins who were the men that did not make it out of Vietnam, replied:

> Oh, that's easy. The optimists. Oh, they were the ones who said, "We're going to be out by Christmas." And Christmas would come, and Christmas would go. Then they'd say, "We're going to be out by Easter." And Easter would come, and Easter would go. And then Thanksgiving, and then it would be Christmas again. And they died of a broken heart.
>
> This is a very important lesson. You must never confuse the faith that you will prevail in the end—which you can never afford to lose—with the discipline to confront the most brutal facts of your current reality, whatever they might be.

Collins called this need to combine faith with confronting the brutal facts the "Stockdale paradox."

Frankl differed from conventional psychotherapists who saw a person's choices in life as coming from their habitual response to the past, in that he saw the potential future as ultimately what determined a person's decisions. In *Man's Search for Meaning*, he gives the example of a Nazi doctor who was particularly callous and brutal. At the end of the war, the Nazi was kidnapped and imprisoned by the Soviets. Suddenly, the heartless man changed his stripes and became a veritable saint to his fellow prisoners, most of whom were completely unaware of his heartless past.

To Frankl, pathological behavior is that which prevents one from experiencing meaning. From his perspective, escapism, compulsiveness, and denial are problematic. Therefore, the role of the therapist is not to analyze the patient but to ask the right questions, so that the patient him or herself can find the meaning in it. He noted Nietzsche's saying, *He who has a "why" can endure any "how."* Clearly, Frankl's experience in that Nazi camp proved Nietzsche's words to be so.

One example of Frankl's method highlights his approach in a particularly moving fashion. He relates the story of an elderly physician who came to him for treatment of depression a few years after the man's beloved wife had died. Frankl listened to his story without comment or analysis. Finally, he offered him a question: "How would your wife have fared if you had been the one who died first?"

The doctor responded, "Oh, it would have crushed her. She would have suffered immensely."

Frankl replied, "Then can you see that by surviving her, you have spared her terrible sorrow?"

The doctor thought about it for some time. Then he slowly stood and smiled. "Thank you, Doctor," he said and shook Frankl's hand. He left Frankl's office, shoulders erect, never to return.

Let us consider for a moment the alternatives that Frankl could have but did not choose, that a more conventional, less brilliant mind might have offered the troubled doctor. Many therapists might have offered advice, such as make more friends, get exercise, get involved, let go of the past. Others might have tried to delve into the man's past to see why his grieving was so intense for him, perhaps even prying into his relationship with his mother. Perhaps they would have explored his relationship with his wife. More modern therapists might encourage him to explore meditation as a treatment for his depression. But all of this comes from the view that the patient is doing something wrong and needs to be corrected, as if that would help.

Sadly, the most common response today would be to prescribe medication, the biggest "fix" of all, depriving the patient of any chance of extracting value from his suffering. Even more, the medication approach would condition the man even further to believe there was something wrong with him for suffering and to see his pain as a reminder of his failure to cope. Instead, Frankl offered his patient what was essentially a solution to his problem, one that did not make him wrong for having the problem, but took what the man valued most and made it into a reason for continuing to live, taking his weakness and making it into a strength. For now his suffering had a meaning: he was enduring it so his beloved wife did not have to.

By now, you can understand how meaning is extremely important, but there is more to it. As I said at the beginning of this discussion, I do think it is because meanings create values. Values are deep determinants of attitudes and interests, which lead to desires. How you look at the world and what you look for determine what you see and how you evaluate things. It is often only after that evaluation that you decide what you want. To give an example, two people may experience the same sexual desires, but if one lives in a world where the meaning of those desires is temptation by the devil and eternal damnation, he or she may be more likely to mortify the flesh than indulge it.

I have talked to a number of people who could be called "cult survivors" or refugees from a particular group of fellow-believers. Even more traumatic for these people than leaving their friends behind when exiting the cult, is losing the world-view and meaning of life that was shared in that group. The person now feels alone and adrift in a world where nothing is known for certain. Anyone who hasn't left the world of larger society for a cult with a contrary world view and then returned alone cannot imagine the particular kind of existential quandary that person faces. Perhaps the closest parallels are immigrants or returning veterans, but despite those individuals' unique tribulations and even traumas, neither face doubting the ultimate meaning of life that the ex-cultist faces.

WHY BOTHER?

You may be asking yourself why you should bother with all this talk of meaning. You may even have started to wonder, over the course of our discussion on happiness, why you should try to improve yourself at all. Why not simply be content with whatever life throws at you?

The answer is because you can't—being content is simply not that easy. As Epictetus pointed out in the *Handbook*, our tendency is to fight battles, even the those that we cannot possible win. Buddhism offers the added insight that life has a nasty habit of taking away even the things that one possesses, an insight also shared by Epictetus. Effort to improve one's self is necessary just to meet those battles and emotionally survive.

Okay, you might ask, *but why not just medicate yourself— and get through life that way?* Of course, quite a lot of people try just that. The problem is that medication isn't dependable, has side-effects, and over time becomes ineffective as you get used to it. Sooner or later, you are going to have to wise up to the fact that life is posing a question for you to answer. And that question is about what it all means.

Which brings us back, via this discussion on meaning, to a question I left you hanging about in an earlier chapter, as you may recall, the topic of contentment. With your understanding now of the importance of meaning, this question takes on new meaning: *Why is it that some people are content with less than others?*

The answer of course is multi-fold. One reason is that some people's disposition is less driven than others. They could also have differing psychological histories and family backgrounds. Ultimately, what isn't explained by their constitutions is probably explained by the difference in their values. Some people value material things, some value spiritual things, and some even value contentment in its own right.

But whatever values people have, as I've said, those values are determined by the meaning and beliefs that are important to them. Some are even willing to undergo extreme hardship in pursuit of their meaning. Such persons who come to mind are Nelson Mandela, the founder of modern democratic South Africa, and Mahatma Gandhi, both of whom endured long prison spells in pursuit of their visions, as well as many lesser known individuals who endured other or similar sacrifices. I saw an interview with Aung San Suu Ky, the Burmese leader who was imprisoned for nearly two decades and was in 2012 seeking election for the nation's Presidency. Interviewer Ann Curry asked her if it was difficult to lose her freedom and be separated from her loved ones for so long. She answered that it was harder for her family than it was for her, because she was always clear on what her life's purpose was. The point is that no matter what a person's meaning may be, when it is well understood, it adds to their resilience and forbearance under hardship.

Finally, in response to the "why bother?" question, I would say that self-improvement is a worthy goal. Intuitively, it seems obviously better to meet life on the offensive than on the defensive. Ideally, it should improve your outlook and self-esteem by increasing your abilities in the future as well as your optimism about facing the future. The real point is to use self-improvement not as an addictive mechanism for pursuing fantasies and dreams, but to pursue new avenues and develop new talents with its aid. And that takes some reflection about meaning and values, because they are what determine whether your direction is forward or just in a circle.

HOW TO KILL A DEPRESSION

Now we are going to get to the part I've been promising you all along, but I need to tell you how it all transpired.

One fateful morning, I lay on my floor despairing, as I had been for weeks. As I tried everything I knew to get out of my depression, my frustration came to a climax. For the first time, I was ready to look at life as brutally realistically as Frankl and Admiral Stockdale advised, and as I myself had resolved in the Carson City hotel room the year before when I began to question previously accepted "truths." (At this point, I'd not yet read Frankl, only coming to him accidentally—or synchronistically, if you will—on my own nearly a year later.)

Frustrated that nothing I was doing seemed to penetrate my depression, I decided to make one more attempt to get out of it. I ran through my mind thinking of every solution I had ever learned in every therapy office, workshop, book or whatever. I tried meditating, expressing my feelings, dialoguing with my inner child, sleeping, visualizing. I tried accepting my feelings, labeling them, seeing them as different colors—you name it. But all of this only made it worse. Then, since nothing was working to make me feel better, and in complete desperation, I decided to see if I couldn't make myself feel *worse*.

Suddenly the feelings of despair completely vanished. After a moment, I realized why. The key was in what I had written in jest to a friend nearly a year before: "Since trying never works, why don't you try to be *un*happy, and see if that works?" But now, it was actually true. I tried to recreate the bad feelings I'd been swamped with only moments before but was unable to recreate them. I tried to feel all sorts of other negative feelings, but they were just as inaccessible. In fact, they were as inaccessible to me now as happiness had been just moments before! I was now happy in spite of myself—and for no damn reason I could explain.

In the weeks following, I experimented with this technique of trying to be unhappier many times and found that it nearly always worked. One big exception was with the emotion of anger. At first, I wondered if anger was somehow a different order of emotion and required different handling, but I came to realize that wasn't so. My difficulty was that because I tended to repress my anger, feeling feel anger doubly strong only served to release pent up feelings that had been repressed earlier—making me feel, well, *angrier*. Once I realized what was happening, I could simply let it be, not feeling anger doubly strong and not stuffing it either, because the last thing I wanted to do with my magic technique was have it become an excuse for repression.

In the days following my breakthrough with depression, I found it to be as if my intelligence had increased, and my ability to respond to inner situations had become magnified. I responded to emotional pain in a quite different way. Instead of asking myself what was wrong with me, as I so often did in my spiraling depression, I reasoned thus: *The purpose of life is to learn. The way we learn is by suffering. Ergo, when I am suffering, I am just doing my job!* The simple logic made me laugh, but it also made me see the value and meaning in my pain, which I could now appreciate and thus lift myself from the hopelessness and despair I'd been in. This turned out to be a second insight, which I will explain in the paragraph after next.

Then, I briefly hit a day where my depression seemed to be returning. At first, when I tried my new methods and they didn't seem to work, I started to panic. The thought occurred to me that maybe I didn't have the answer after all, which was even more depressing. But then the thought came to me, *If I don't have the answer, wouldn't I want to know that, and as quickly as possible?* The answer was yes, again confirming that I was on the right track. And then the thought came, *Well, the only thing that's going on now is that I am doing more research.* In other words, I'm not doing anything wrong, but rather I'm doing something right!

Some readers may recognize my method as a psychological technique known as *re-framing*. In re-framing, you change the meaning of a situation from a negative one to a positive one. The more positive meaning, however, must be something that is believable, not something you are straining to believe. The key is how you feel when you speak the reframing, hearing it as something that is actually *true*. It seems that Frankl was an early discoverer of that technique in his effort to give a positive meaning to his horrific experience in the Nazi camp. Had he not fully embraced his belief, he might never have made it out of the camp.

But why did my technique work? One reason could be the phenomenon I discussed in Chapter 3 on the unconscious. In discussing memory, I noted that recall is often difficult when you are trying to remember something, but that the elusive memory often rises to consciousness unbidden, only after you have moved on to another subject. That may be part of the answer, because I was "moving on" emotionally by using my technique, rather than getting hung up on *trying*, perhaps in the same way as letting go of trying to remember allows you to actually remember something.

Another reason for my technique's success comes from one of Victor Frankl's more interesting observations, resulting in a phenomenon he called *paradoxical intention*.

PARADOXICAL INTENTION

Frankl observed that paranoid behavior, for example, can sometimes be a self-fulfilling prophecy. Frankl wrote in *Man's Search for Meaning* that **"fear brings about that which one is afraid of, and that hyper-intention makes impossible what one wishes."** In other words, the act of trying to directly control a fear or compulsion can trigger a type of anticipatory anxiety which actually has the effect of bolstering the fear or compulsion and making it stronger.

To dispel this sort of neurotic behavior, Frankl devised the technique of *paradoxical intention*, which is a conscious stepping out of the paranoid behavior at hand. Two examples will suffice to demonstrate the nature of this technique. Frankl writes in *Man's Search for Meaning* about the first one:

> *A young physician consulted me because of his fear of perspiring. Whenever he expected an outbreak of perspiration, this anticipatory anxiety was enough to precipitate excessive sweating. In order to*

> *cut this circle formation, I advised the patient, in the event that sweating should recur, to resolve deliberately to show people how much he could sweat.*
>
> *A week later he returned to report that whenever he met anyone who triggered his anticipatory anxiety, he said to himself, "I only sweated out a quart before, but now I'm going to pour out at least ten quarts!"*
>
> *The result was that, after suffering from his phobia for four years, he was able, after a single session, to free himself permanently of it within one week.*

In a second example, he writes:

> *Paradoxical intention can also be applied in cases of sleep disturbance. The fear of sleeplessness results in a hyper-intention to fall asleep, which in turn, incapacitates the patient to do so. To overcome this particular fear, I usually advise the patient to do just the opposite, that is, to stay awake as long as possible.*
>
> *In other words, the hyper-intention to fall asleep, arising from the anticipatory anxiety of not being able to do so, must be replaced by the paradoxical intention not to fall asleep, which soon will be followed by sleep.*

Of course, one must also be cautious to not fall into the trap of trying to stay awake *in order* to fall asleep, which would be quite self-defeating. It has to be an intention that has no agenda, because "trying" to become detached will only result in sabotage.

Put another way, by turning your fears and compulsions on their heads, you can cut off the anticipatory anxiety that triggers and reinforces those fears, thereby diffusing them in a sort of a reverse psychology tactic. Frankl also noticed that the act of trying to increase problematic situations made the approach a bit humorous. He noted that in most cases, to find a situation as humorous was the beginning of the end of its power over a person. He quotes Gordon Allport, who said in his book, *The Individual and His Religion*, that "The neurotic who learns to laugh at himself may be on the way to self-management, [even] to a cure..."

But as I continued to experiment, I found that there were occasions during which I had neither the time nor the desire to go into a negative emotion so deeply, as is needed in Frankl's paradoxical intention. Often, I simply noticed that I was trying to feel good (and failing), or trying *not* to feel bad (and also failing). Sometimes that simple realization that I was trying to do something that could only fail (in my view) was enough to help me relax and let go of whatever was bothering me.

One time I was sitting in a meeting fidgeting and making myself uncomfortable when I suddenly realized that I was trying not to feel bored. That was going to be a fruitless task, for sure, especially considering how much I hate meetings. Finally, I said to myself, *I am glad I am bored.* That certainly felt better than being frustrated with myself over feeling bored. It felt stronger than saying to myself, *I understand how I could be bored,* or *I accept myself being bored,* or many of the other things I might have thought to say. I went on from there: *How could I not be bored? This meeting is TOTALLY boring. I'm even bored with being bored!*

All of a sudden, I could see that I was practicing a version of Frankl's technique of paradoxical intention that was also based on my own original discovery. But now I had a short cut, which was skipping getting into the emotion deeply, and instead, more than accepting it, actually welcoming and in fact, congratulating myself on it. You will recall my earlier discussion on complaints and congratulations, so I hope you can see that turning this complaint into an authentic congratulations could have a big benefit.

As I have explained this discovery on several occasions to friends, some have remarked that I am simply practicing gratitude, a favorite recommendation of New Age teachers these days. Technically that may be true, but I am doing gratitude with a twist. A New Age teacher would recommend I practice gratitude *about* the situation, as in trying to accept it and being grateful for it in some way. However, I am practicing gratitude for my emotion, not the situation I am in, and that important difference prevents me from being in conflict with my experience.

A Buddhist teacher I explained my method to responded by saying I was practicing *non-resistance*, a Buddhist technique of accepting what you cannot change. But again, it is only true with the twist that emphasizes emotion over situation. Because if one *tries* to practice non-resistance regarding a situation, it is all too easy to end up actually resisting one's own resistance. And in this case "the enemy of my enemy" is not my friend! I am not non-resisting a particular situation or circumstance, I am only non-resisting my feelings. Another way to say that is that I am getting on the same side as my feelings.

In Chapter 2 on emotions, I explained that not only do we have emotions, but we have thoughts and feelings about our emotions. These thoughts and feelings end up being quite significant, in that our internal environment is always closer to us than the external environment. So I ask you, which will be more uncomfortable: resisting your internal environment or resisting the external one? The internal environment is actually closer, so therefore likely to be affecting us more strongly.

You might suggest that resisting neither would be even better, and I would agree. But I would also say, why make life hard? If you can lower the conflict in any arena, why not do it? In any case, the purpose is not emotional repression, which is ultimately unhealthy, but simply to manage one's emotions. For example, if a person close to me dies, I would not try to feel grateful about the situation—which would be weird—but I'm fine with feeling *glad* that I am grieving, therefore not resisting my grief. To respond this way simply makes me normal. So the purpose, again, is not to be a super-human robot but a healthy human being who feels his or her emotions in an appropriate way.

In addition to being glad, there has to be a good reason for saying so, hence the second phrase after "I am glad," which provides the support and rationale and makes it believable. In the beginning, I was explaining my gladness or non-resistance in terms of "just doing my job," and later that "it's normal to feel this way." It strikes me that the specific content is not crucial to its success and that whatever is meaningful to the individual at the time is appropriate. It may be good to start with the "it's normal" theme, but one's own genius will provide others, if they are appropriate or needed.

Some people may object that my approach, coming at the end of the whole thought/feeling chain of events, seems a little like the tail wagging the dog (as the phrase goes.) It's true that unlike most self-help, it is working at the back end of thoughts and feelings, rather than at the front. But that is why it doesn't run afoul of Wegner's *ironic processes*. No thoughts or feelings need to be suppressed.

I mentioned the debate in Chapter Three over whether thoughts cause feelings or the reverse, but pointed out that the real issue was where to intervene. It seems that that answer is after both of them. So rather than the tail wagging the dog, it is more like a rudder steering a ship. Of course, a rudder is always at the back of the ship for a good reason. It is the place where the least amount of effort has the maximum result. Steering the ship from the front would be far harder. So rather than wasting effect suppressing our thoughts and feelings, we catch them on the back end and turn them around by reducing the conflict they create.

Another way to look at how paradoxical intention works is through the concept I introduced in the previous chapter, the *coherent energy field*. Our mental and emotional selves are constantly stirred up by conflicting thoughts and feelings, creating a non-coherent energy field. When Frankl prescribed paradoxical intention for his patients, he was reducing conflict by getting them to do more of what they already couldn't help doing. What that did was release the conflict, producing a coherent field going in the opposite direction.

I bring up this point especially for those who are more spiritually than psychologically oriented, and who may doubt the value of psychological exercises. In other words, I am trying to explain that paradoxical intention is achieving the same goal of peaceful coherent energy but in a different way, one that may be easier to achieve than by using positive thinking or conventional spiritual practices.

Similarly, from Daniel Wegner's perspective of *ironic processes*, you may recall from Chapter 1 that there are two main mental activities, the "operating" principle and the "monitoring" principle. Normally the two should work together, but under stress (whether short-term or longer) the operating principle is weakened and the monitoring principle overtakes it, creating sabotage of one's efforts. With paradoxical intention however, the operating principle can be doing the same thing as the monitoring principle, short-circuiting that pattern of sabotage.

For example, normally the operating principle tries to accomplish a simple function like going to sleep. Under stress, the monitoring principle kicks in and repeatedly is checking: *Am I falling asleep, am I falling asleep now?* Of course, under those circumstances sleep may be impossible. In the case where Frankl's patient overcame his insomnia, it was because he stopped trying to sleep and started trying to stay awake, which, any student will tell you, is the first thing to make you sleepy when you are staying up to study—if, that is, you don't have an artificial stimulant to help you stay awake.

Frankl notes that paradoxical intention is not a panacea, which means it is not going to work all the time for all people. If it were, I think, it would have two faults. First, it would become a tool of repression, helping one not to feel, and second, it would become an obstacle to meaning, preventing one from thinking. But if paradoxical intention is not a panacea, an infallible cure, then what is it? To me, it is a tool to free the mind and allow one's genius to be set free.

Ultimately, in Frankl's view, the need is to find a meaning for living, whatever that might be to that individual in that moment, to be happy. You may recall that in Chapter 2, I mentioned that there were two kinds of contentment: one that depended on satisfied desires, and a second more dynamic one that was related to a goal larger than oneself. That is what Frankl was attempting to explain by emphasizing having a purpose larger than oneself. For him, it was ultimately a spiritual quality, whether the goal was something in this world or another. The meaning could be found in another person, a cause, a belief system, or anything that has value to the specific person. This is why helping others is often a source of fulfillment for some.

IMPLICATIONS AND APPLICATIONS

There are some important implications of Frankl's writings for therapy and self help.

First, regarding positive thinking, we can add another criticism to the already long list. A person who practices positive thinking is trying to simply replace negative thoughts with positive ones. Even if it did work, it has the net effect of inhibiting introspection. There is only one thing that anyone is ever doing wrong, in their view, and it is thinking negatively. Such a superficial view inhibits true problem-solving and learning from mistakes. It also inhibits the possible discovery of meaning, since in that view positivity is the only meaning there is.

Regarding therapy, while a therapist should accept a client's world view, he or she should not be afraid to confront clients to the extent of helping them look for a further meaning. Reactions to events do not need to necessarily be analyzed and connected to the past unless they are clearly out of proportion to current circumstances. A realistic and honest appraisal should always be given. Promises about future progress should never be made. I feel this is extremely important. It is borne out by the logic of this book which shows how the fantasy of improvement can be an immediate producer of "happiness," even if a false hope. But as Frankl pointed out, false hopes and/or expectations for improvement lead inevitably to disillusionment which in the end sabotages any attempts at therapy.

It's may be tempting to a therapist, whenever leaving a client in the emotional disarray of stirred up emotion, to reward the client for their session by saying "That was important work." But the problem with such rewards is the client may take it as an implied promise of improvement. It might be preferable from a long-term point of view to get into the habit of returning the client to a neutral state rather than a positive one that could set up an expectation of the future.

Finally, whether this is applied to therapy, coaching, or self-help, overly exercising the will should be approached with caution to prevent "hyper-intentionality." This warning is supported by my insights on the perils of "trying," as such a reaction can occur in even as an apparently harmless thing as trying to change a bad habit.

Here's an example: A friend recently consulted with an expert on controlling his weight. The first advice he was given was to stop dieting. Most overweight people, as you may know, get into an endless cycle of deprivation and indulging, and end up yoyo-ing – one of the worst possible outcomes in terms of health. Instead, the expert encouraged my friend to pay attention to his diet and learn what caused him to binge, as well as providing him with hints to make small lifestyle changes that avoided extremes. Overly exercising the will did not play a part in the expert's expert advice.

Sometimes, as a friend who is asked to give advice, I find myself falling into the trap I'm warning against. When I finished my first draft of this manuscript, I showed it to a friend and asked him for an opinion. He said that he liked it but wasn't sure how to create more emotional distance in his life. At first, I started to answer, "Well, you can talk to someone outside the situation, go for a walk, meditate..." But then I stopped. "That's what everyone else will tell you, but in the end, even though it is good advice, all it will do is cause more trying and thus more conflict."

I told him that better was to get out of that trap of trying once and for all, which is where the approach of saying *I'm GLAD I feel _____* . (fill in the blank) comes in. It is an intervention into the thought emotion process that validates rather than invalidates. Maybe it helps you laugh at yourself or maybe not, but what it does do for certain is reduce the internal conflict that results from trying.

Interestingly, the reduction in conflict and the increase in validation does seem to improve the "distance," not through the usual method of going to the other extreme of repression or distraction from one's feelings, but by moving a small increment closer to the center. It is also turning a complaint into a congratulation, a key moment that I addressed in Chapter 2.

I recall an incident where a friend of mine was complaining that she couldn't convince her sister to take action to change her life, and that she was frustrated by the sister's continual complaining. My friend had even tried complaining back to her sister about the burden her frustration was causing her. After explaining and venting about the story for a while, she asked me for advice.

I tried the typical psychologist's technique of turning it back to her with a question, "What do *you* think you should do?" but got the perfectly reasonable response, "I have no idea—that's *why* I am asking you!"

Instead of following Epictetus and advising her to stop trying to change something she had no control over, i.e. another person's actions, I tried to ease her into the tactic I was using on myself.

I asked, "Do you feel it is wrong to be frustrated with your sister?"

She responded, "No, it just *is* frustrating! Don't you think that's normal?"

"Of course, it's normal," I replied. "Can you at least be glad that you are having a normal reaction?" She looked at me quizzically for a minute and then said, "Well, it's better than trying *not* to have a reaction."

So I said, "Why don't you try saying, *I'm GLAD I am frustrated with my sister...*"

(Students of Re-evaluation Counseling will recognize this approach as being very similar to a *contradiction*, the technique I briefly described in Chapter 3.)

My friend said the statement a couple of times and then starting laughing, "Hell, yes, it's normal. Of course I would feel frustrated. I'm *glad* I'm frustrated. It's perfectly normal to get frustrated when someone you care about never listens to you and then ruins their life. That just means I'm normal."

But being "normal" isn't the point, as the following anecdote illustrates. I remember having one of those incidents in traffic that even the most enlightened of us are subject to. The fellow in the other car did something that seemed reasonable to him, I suppose, but not to me. Under the pressure of being in a hurry and feeling frustrated, I engaged in a little macho behavior by speeding up along side of him. After leaving his car behind me flames (at least in my mind!), I put away my rocket launcher and a little further down the road started to feel funny.

That wasn't normal behavior, I thought uncomfortably. *Well, I'm GLAD I wasn't normal*, I thought in response. *Who wants to be normal anyway?* That relieved the pressure of my feelings which then allowed me after a few minutes to descend into the next level, which was that I felt guilty.

But I kept on applying the method: *I'm GLAD I feel guilty – that just means I'm not a complete sociopath!*

Occasionally, even the repetition of "gladulations" —what I have come to call this process of congratulating myself on my natural reactions—doesn't work all the time. Although that is rare, when it doesn't, I have my fallback technique, which is to dive into the Full Monty, as it were, of trying to feel the emotion twice as strongly, which might sound like this in my thoughts: *I am feel totally guilty, I am so guilty, guilty, guilty. GUILTY! I Just pronounce me guilty as charged!* Once said, I feel the emotion wash over me and move out, as my stomach relaxes, and I find myself taking a deep breath. But be warned, as I mentioned about anger, this may not happen with an emotion you have repressed a lot. You just may need to feel it enough to get into balance. But what I can report is that once that happens, then this method works well, and you may even hear a little voice saying…*I'm glad I feel…*

Of course, this is not the final end of the matter. If you not getting what you want and remain frustrated, then it is likely that an emotion will eventually return, but at least you have not glossed it over with repression, distraction, or a spiritual bypass, and so added one more layer of BS on top of it.

And that's where the search for meaning comes in. I realized from my friend's comment above about not knowing how to create emotional distance, that I needed to emphasize the power of this technique more, and that it really does work. On the other hand, I did not want to turn it into a kind of religion or philosophy, because that would inhibit the search for meaning, which is ultimately what we need for growth as individuals.

A similar implication can be made for the average person regarding self improvement. We are always trying to find a "winning formula." Nearly all self-help books fall into that category. But if there is a winning formula, then human life has been reduced to the merely mechanical. We could be taught the method as children and apply it throughout life. But as is human nature, through repetition we become accustomed to things. What was once good or worked becomes boring, or doesn't work. And what was bad, becomes tolerable.

Why does this happen? It is due to a change in reference points. After a time, we stop comparing the current situation to an earlier one, and replace the earlier one with one nearer in time. In fact, it can be generally said, that nothing seems good or bad except in comparison to something else. Even a person who loses a leg might feel good about it, if the alternative is losing *both* legs. A loved one's death normally provokes grief but could provoke relief if the loved one's suffering were too great. Even the prospect of our own imminent demise could be seen positively with faith that as a believer one was going to heaven.

On the other hand, as people age, they develop a kind of maturity where many things, especially the small ones, start to be seen in perspective. The only thing that may prevent that natural maturing is our inability to learn and find meaning in ordinary life because of obstacles like distraction, obsessive thinking, repression and, of course, addictions.

I am proposing a technique, not a solution. Once we free our minds to solve our problems, the problems still do need to be solved. But again, with our minds freed, our problems are often more easily resolved.

SOMETIMES THE LESSON IN LIFE IS...

It was a cloudy, windy day in central California. I don't remember the exact date, but it was in the year or so before the Carson City hotel room epiphany and the discovery of my version of paradoxical intention. It was a depressing day, and I felt it. I was alone.

I decided to get some fresh air and go for a walk on a nearby deserted beach. I bundled up a little and drove to the beach, and then walked and walked and walked. Eventually I got tired of walking and lay down on top of a picnic table, stretching out and watching the clouds. I began reflecting on my life and all the decisions I made. Starting at about age 17, I thought about every decision I'd made that year I could remember. Of course, a lot of them were not bad decisions, but there were plenty of regrets and mistakes. I was already in a bad mood, so masochistically I decided to keep going, looking at all the mistakes I had made the next year at age 18. And then the next, and the next. With each year of reflection, my mood got worse, and with it my masochism. So I kept on going. Eventually I got to my current age and from there looked back on a lifetime of mistakes.

Oddly, I didn't feel the least bit suicidal. In fact, I remember just shrugging and thinking, *Well, I guess those were my lessons in life.* I suppose that response was a precursor to my discovery of my version of paradoxical intention. In truth, it was pretty courageous of me, if I may say so, to keep looking at myself without blinking. In fact, it gave me some solace in the tough months that were ahead to know I'd done some real work and also reframed a lot of negative memories and regrets.

But there came a day, sometime after my breakthrough, when the inspiration my discovery had left me no longer inspired. In fact, as I sorted through my thoughts and feelings about a recent situation (the content of which I no longer remember) and tried to extract a lesson from it, I was struck by all the different ways I had been taught to look at this problem from various self-help books, psychologists and spiritual teachers. I felt a bit of a quandary. There were so many possible lessons and no way to decide which one was the right one. The thought occurred to me, *Sometimes the lesson in life is to learn what the lesson in life is.*

Of course, that made me laugh, but it also hit a deep chord, which is this: In the end, any meaning gained from any source outside yourself is artificial; and you can't necessarily *try* to find meaning any better than you can try at anything else. But what you can do is be willing to look at your life and be open to understanding the meaning when things are ready to fall into place.

So we are now coming full circle. We started with the world's first self-help book, Epictetus' *Handbook*, and conclude by updating it with modern psychology, spirituality, and Viktor Frankl's wisdom about meaning in life. Let's see in the next chapter how it all fits together—and even if it can.

The stakes are rather high: If we can fit it together we have a path to a better life for both the thinking person and the average person. If we cannot, then we've poked holes in all the current choices but been unable to offer a real alternative.

CHAPTER 8

PUTTING *MOST OF IT* TOGETHER

There comes a time, whether you are building a jigsaw puzzle, playing "Hangman" on a cocktail napkin, or writing a book, when you have to step back and look at the big picture in order to finish the job. So let's take a look at what we've covered so far.

We've seen how happiness appears to be both a feeling and state of mind, based primarily on two things: perceived circumstances and expectations. In addition, some factors can influence us from both above and below—spirituality and the unconscious.

I started out by reminding us that the pursuit of happiness often fails, simply because it raises expectations without necessarily providing the pursuer with the ability to change circumstances. Epictetus addresses the problem by advising us only to fight the battles in life that we can win. However, life is often itself literally a battle, and it requires more self-control than many of us have. This was an argument made against Epictetus's approach even back in ancient times.

We have looked at positive thinking, which proposes the simple solution of just jumping into *being* happy instead of chasing after it. This sounds fine on paper but runs afoul of Daniel Wegner's ironic processes, which sabotages the solution completely for many people and for many others when they most need a solution - *at least as it is conventionally practiced* - as well as being problematic for the other reasons I've discussed.

Next we looked at the emotions. Here we came across a couple of important clues: the ideas of reflexive emotions and the difference between pain and suffering. We can untangle the layers of complex emotions, and though we can't avoid pain, we can at least theoretically reduce suffering by not personalizing and generalizing it into beliefs about ourselves, God or life. Unfortunately, even untangling emotions and expressing them, while it reduces the pressure of emotions, fails to resolve the chronic frustrations of deep-seated issues, so we were forced to look deeper at the role of the unconscious.

In the deep unconscious, (the existence of which was proved, I hope, to your satisfaction), we found the keys to understanding suffering and sabotage. Unfortunately, although the keys fit, they did not fully turn the lock, since only *some* of those deep seated issues could be cured. Additionally, from the point of view of our exploration, we can see how therapy, while useful, can backfire. There, the result is to confuse some people by constantly reminding them of painful issues, by implicitly comparing them to a "healthy" standard, and by making them frustrated with not changing fast enough.

And so we considered reversing course - following in the footsteps of the humanistic psychologists into loftier realms of ultimate meaning, leading to New Age spirituality. Here, too, we found a way to turn the key a little more by opening up to "higher" influences, but the door remained only partially open, not fully. And here also lay dangers. From our analysis, we can see how spirituality can confuse people and promote unhappiness by making spiritual perfection a standard to which they compare themselves. We noted other pitfalls along the spiritual path, such as people becoming tantalized with spiritual experiences they may not be able to access, having other potential meanings invalidated, and finally by people being encouraged to see others as spiritually superior and thus get exploited by false spiritual teachers.

Lastly, we turned to Viktor Frankl, who reminded us of the power of meaning and how that meaning is actively discovered by the individual and never passively received from outer sources. He also introduced us to the concept of paradoxical intention as a possible remedy for ironic processes, which I have illustrated with both my own personal stories and those of people I know.

But after now having reviewed all this, I would imagine you to be suspicious of any simplistic solution. The question then is, can we put it all together to come up with something to works for living a better life?

First, let's go back to Epictetus. When I think of the problem that there is no instant cure-all, I have to imagine Epictetus as having a good laugh. He would say, "I *told* you that there are things you simply have to accept." And we have been learning that is true, even for those things that occur inside us. Although Epictetus would have approved of some of their goals, I'm pretty certain he would have little patience for people driving themselves crazy by trying to improve themselves or thinking themselves rich. Rather, a sober patience is more what he would preach to those who were attempting to change, whether inside or out.

You may have noticed in the title of this chapter I alluded to putting *most* and not all of it together. There is a reason why we probably cannot put it *all* together, and that is because life is always changing, and we are always changing. As another Greek philosopher by the name of Heraclitus put it, "No man steps twice into the same river." The river is always changing, and so is the man. (Nowadays, we even object that the saying uses "man" instead of "person!") So if you think there are eternal truths, well, I would say yes, but only in the eternal realm. Life is open-ended, and if my understanding and society's cannot be improved, then it is probably because we have reached a dead end, so there always will be new challenges to master.

It is important to understand that as with life, emotions also have their ups and downs. Obviously, I am not one who prescribes finding happiness in all circumstances. Instead, I have offered some perspective on the ups and downs of life, so that people do not *decrease* their happiness through self-judgment but instead reap the benefits of the crucible of suffering when it occurs. But that doesn't mean I am giving up or offering something minor when everyone wants something big. In fact, what I will try to do for the remainder of this chapter is offer something *complete* – something that includes all of what you may want to consider – and indeed offers a multiplicity of approaches from different angles. To do that, we must start again from the beginning, this time stressing the issues that inform my conclusions.

PASSION AND POSITIVITY: OPPOSING IDEALS

Each of us is unique in terms of our level of cheerfulness, as I am sure you have observed. But while our society urges us to be happy with who we are, it also urges us "to stay positive." The motivation is obvious: Positive people create fewer waves and so can be more easily controlled, which is why religion has been called the "opiate of the masses." With religion, people are easier to control in the family, church, job and society, because there is less complaining. But control comes as at a cost, which is the moral of Barbara Ehrenreich's *Bright-Sided,* a book I mentioned in Chapter 1. People did try to live with stricter controls at one time, back in the 1950s, but it doesn't work, because too much conformity is stifling.

We are also told, on the other hand, that it is a good thing to be passionate, to express our emotions freely and authentically. No one wants a milquetoast, Pollyanna-type hanging around. However, if passionate means angry and bad-tempered—well, we don't want *that* either.

I am pointing to a contradiction that exists between the ideals of passion and positivity. As in all things, the ideal probably falls somewhere in the middle. But rather than adding another ideal to all the others people try to live up to, I propose a more natural way, which is that we can live more in harmony with our emotions while not completely falling victim to them.

A person who is naturally balanced would be in touch with his or her emotions, feel comfortable with being "negative" occasionally, and still get along with people. There is no one trick to bringing about such a state, but there several strategies for accomplishing it and a number of tactics that are useful. By strategies, I mean long-term projects, and by tactics I mean day-to-day or as-needed actions.

MANAGEMENT VS CONTROL

You have probably heard of the common strategies that are well-known in our society, basic ones like healthful living through diet and exercise, social interaction, and useful work. There are also well-known supplemental strategies, such as spiritual attunement and psychological re-adjustment. A third supplemental strategy is not as common but equally critical, and that is the strategy of *mental self-management*.

For most of people in our society, mental self-management is demonstrated only by positive thinking, as in managing one's thoughts to remain in a narrow range of positivity. But I prefer to follow more in the footsteps of Epictetus by promoting that we manage our thoughts through a discipline of understanding. (I use the word *discipline* in its original meaning as "a practice of learning.") We must learn to understand our minds as the Buddhists teach, life as Epictetus taught, and our emotions and unconscious as psychology demonstrates.

If you understand how your thoughts and emotions work in interaction with life's circumstances, you can better manage them without subjecting them to the strict controls that ultimately backfire. And that management is where any modern approach must ultimately be located. Even in ancient times, stoics like Epictetus were criticized as being too severe. Likewise, in the modern era, Buddhism is considered too dry and pessimistic by many people. And while one cannot satisfy everybody, listening to one's critics can often prove worthwhile.

Furthermore, consider this: After thousands of years of human history, we have not learned how to control our minds, so maybe we should try to accomplish things by another method. That method, which I am proposing, would be to gain greater understanding of the workings of the mind. Ever since Freud's discovery of the unconscious, we have come to understand why it's so difficult to change ourselves. There were earlier explanations for this difficulty, but they were all externalized, as in "the devil made me do it." But now, for the first time, we have the possibility of owning our "dark side" and, if not controlling it, being able to manage it for a happier, more successful life.

Management makes better sense than control. If you own a dog or cat, you know there are certain things you must manage as opposed to eliminate. You unleash the dog sometimes and buy the cat a scratching board, so as not to directly oppose its nature but provide it an outlet instead. The same is true with our own mental and emotional natures. While thoughts and feelings are almost impossible to control, they are manageable with an understanding of their nature.

This is the strategy that I am advising. We have spent the last seven chapters understanding the peculiar nature of the human dilemma. I have shown first why controlling the mind doesn't work, especially for the people who need it most and at the times they need it most. I have also tried to show that the remedies of the modern era—emotional processing and psychological excavation—while useful, are not a full solution. Furthermore, I've attempted to demonstrate that the rediscovery of Eastern philosophy as absorbed into the New Age philosophy, while useful, is also not the full answer. Finally, I've demonstrated how two insights of genius by Viktor Frankl—the importance of meaning and paradoxical intention—when combined with the basic rethinking of our fixation with happiness, give us a fuller understanding of the human being.

Our minds will always project into the future by either fantasizing or worrying. Most people who have meditated for decades still have not accomplished going beyond such projecting. I also know a number of people who have studied Eckhart Tolle's *The Power of Now* for many years with equally modest results. In fact, some are still practicing trying to expand their awareness of the "now" into the future—oxymoronic as that may seem.

Likewise, the nature of our human emotions is reaction. That's the way they are and the way they were designed, so it's probably not very realistic to expect them to cease being that way, either. Instead, I propose we learn some tactics to prevent those natural tendencies from turning into sources of conflict, blame, or depression. One such tactic I've found particularly helpful is to give a new framework to the usual approach of trying.

EXPERIMENTING, NOT EFFORTING

I have mentioned often how trying never works, but here it is useful to distinguish two separate meanings of the word "trying." *Trying* to do something—as Yoda pointed out in *Star Wars*—is not the same as actually *doing* it. That kind of trying is *struggling* to do it, not actually doing it—a thankless task.

On the other hand, to "try out" something, by way of *experimenting*, is a useful tool that can expand your repertoire. With experimenting, a negative result doesn't necessarily mean a failure but rather can be seen simply as an elimination of an approach that doesn't work. So whenever you hear the word "try," including from me, don't think of it as struggling but rather as an invitation to experiment. *Experimenting not efforting*, is the way one friend of mine puts it. The following story illustrates what I mean.

My friend, a critical care nurse, called me while having a meltdown. She complained to me how hard it was, in spite of negative working conditions at her hospital, "to stay positive." Yes, her co-workers were not performing their jobs well, and were adding insult to injury by blaming her for their mistakes. Nothing worked to rectify the problem, not even discussing it with her superiors. In short, she was *trying* to not be negative about a situation she couldn't control, which is exactly as Epictetus might have counseled.

I suggested to my friend that she stop trying and instead simply say what she felt—really venting about it—at least *to herself*. That would be an example of experimenting, as in trying something new. She liked the idea and adopted it, finding that she no longer had to try (as in effort) to do anything (like stay positive). This greatly relieved the inner pressure that was causing additional stress in an already stressful situation. Interestingly, she also became a little more patient with all the problems at work. Obviously, there were more effects for her than for the people around her, as Epictetus would have predicted, but the experiment worked.

This tactic of experimenting rather than efforting fits with the general strategy of mental self-management. Once having gained understanding, you can put that understanding to work—but in a very different way than making efforts to control yourself. Essentially, this is analogous to the difference between a slave owner and a manager. A slave owner will whip, threaten, and punish his slaves into obeying. But slave labor is not an efficient form of production. Slaves seem lazy to the master, because they have no motivation of their own. They even rebel. And that is essentially what happens to you when you "try," as in efforting, to control yourself. You rebel and all efforts are wasted.

Like me, you have probably heard people complain how they would like to be more disciplined in exercise, diet, lifestyle, and yes, even in their practice of positive thinking. When they fail, they think, *I guess I'm just too lazy.* On the other hand, I know many people who are extremely disciplined, work out every day, and eat healthily, and then ruin it all by drinking, taking drugs, smoking, raging, or other addictions. Are these two extremes related? I can't help but think so. Both are products of the tendency to control without fully understanding, as would a slave driver, and therefore end up either flaking or rebelling.

A manager, however, is something different. A manager ideally finds a way to draw out a person's motivations and thereby bring out the best in people. The best managers know how to do this by matching people's talents to their jobs, while finding ways to help them overcome or deflect their weaknesses. That is the strategy I am proposing.

In essence, I am offering this as my perspective: Just as Epictetus reasoned that truly understanding the ups and downs of life allowed us to focus our energy on the things we can affect, I am saying that understanding the ups and downs of our feelings allows us to focus our energy on the thoughts and feelings we can most easily affect – those we have *about* our feelings - those feelings which I have labeled *reflexive feelings*, like guilt and shame. Similarly. too, conclusions (thoughts) about the nature of life, God and ourselves – the very topics I have identified as the causes of suffering (as opposed to simple pain) in an earlier chapter and the emotions that they produce. I have proposed the strategy of paradoxical intention to cope with these as well as any other troublesome feelings.

But I would be remiss in leaving it there, because there are other diamonds that we have discovered during our excavations., and you can benefit from them as well just as long as you don't succumb to the great temptation of self-help; believing your problems will be forever and completely solved. They will not, but what you *do* have is an end to the confusion in how to deal with them.

So here we go…

WRAPPING IT UP

To wrap up our discussion, I'll give you some suggestions to help you apply all of this to your own life, based on insights from the various chapters.

LIFE

You don't need to waste time worrying about things outside of your control (as inspired by Epictetus). These include your age and socio-economic status, election results, the future of the planet, and others' opinions of you and what you have done in the past. Whenever you start to worry about something, consider whether you have any control over it, and if not, stop worrying (or try to worry twice as much – but I am jumping ahead!). Instead, choose the kind of person you want to be and live as much as you can according to those values. If you fail, at least you know you are *trying*. [ha-ha, I mean experimenting!]

You don't need to be defensive with other people. Acknowledge your faults and laugh it off; after all, they may not even know about the rest of your faults. If you find you *are* being defensive, acknowledge it and laugh that off, too. (You may want to laugh on the inside, so as not to seem rude.)

HAPPINESS

Check in with yourself to see what you are feeling. We often carry around an assortment of mixed emotions, none of which can be processed until they are made conscious. A daily inventory of *What am I happy about?/What am I unhappy about?* can keep you current and emotionally healthier than ignoring emotions. In fact, I find this is a surprisingly powerful technique in its own right. Typically, we go through the day feeling a little good or bad. If it's good, fine – but if you are feeling bad, it's good to know why to be able to start the resolution process. Sometimes, I ask people why they are depressed, and they tell me they don't know. When I ask "Well, what are you happy about and what are you unhappy about?" they can begin to think about solutions and/or acceptance and at the very least have a chance to vent. Once you've understand the rest of this book, I've noticed just getting clear on this is often enough to move on.

Remember, in the same way that if you are happy, it may just be a fantasy; if you feel unhappy, it may just represent a worry. You can influence your experience in the moment by altering your reference point to something that is more under your control. Or you can just go with it and "enjoy" (haha) it.

Even if you are *not* currently getting what you want, you also may be *not* getting a lot of things you *don't* want. Remembering the latter will make you feel better than only paying attention to the former. But don't get into trying to replace the unhappiness with happiness—let your mind do it on its own.

It's not in the nature of life to be happy all the time. When you are feeling unhappy, you are not a failure; it's just life. Remember that feeling good and doing well are *not* the same. Never judge yourself for your happiness or lack of it.

Nothing is good or bad except as compared to something else. If you compare your circumstances to something better, you will feel bad; if you compare them to something worse, you will feel good. It's that simple.

It is okay to worry, but beyond a certain point it has no effect. It is okay to fantasize, but beyond a certain point it does no good. Some things are better left as fantasies than turning them into realities. Remember, what *is* making you happy is mostly not the reality, but rather the fantasy you are having of it.

If your pain has turned into suffering, notice what you are saying to yourself about life, God or you. Those conclusions, not based on any fact, are what hold you down—not the things themselves.

Remember that some suffering is normal as we adjust our beliefs about ourselves and God and life to reality. It is the reflexive suffering that is really unnecessary.

EMOTIONS

After checking in on your happiness state, you may want to go further with your emotions. What are you feeling? If it is mixed or complex, there are likely two or occasionally more things going on. You may need to express these emotions to someone in an appropriate manner. People outside the situation are best, preferably people who won't judge you or give you advice (unless you ask).

Just as everyone else has a good reason to feel the way they do, so do you. I think you can see how both your feelings and others' are logical, based on the past and on expectations. Feelings always make sense, but sometimes the perceptions they are based on may turn out to be erroneous.

You have a choice as to what you *do* about your feelings. First, you do not need to act on them. If you feel you must, act in the least harmful possible way to yourself and others. If you do act on them, you may want to mitigate the effects as soon as possible.

What's done is done, and while it is okay to regret something you did, remember your regret will have no effect. The only purpose of regret is to give yourself notice about what not to do next time.

Pay attention to your reflexive feelings. Are you feeling frustrated, guilty or ashamed of is the feelings that are going on inside you?

If you can't be glad about your circumstances, be glad that you have the feelings you do. Always try to get on the same side as your feelings.

Feelings that are OK and normal include gloating, envying, non-forgivingness are other unpopular emotions. Whatever they are you need to feel them, vent them (a little) and even appreciate them perhaps through "gladulations" (Saying "I'm glad that…").

Remember the goal can never be to eliminate all pain, only to reduce suffering. Don't beat yourself up if you feel bad, it's ok, just see whether you can reduce it. I will talk more about this in a couple of pages.

THE UNCONSCIOUS

Everything that happened to you is recorded somewhere, and it is influencing you to some degree, whether you know it or not

Many of your current feelings are triggered by past experiences. We tend to repeat those experiences, even if they are negative.

Negative repetitive experiences are normal. Everyone has them. They don't need to be causes of self-judgment or frustration.

If you have a strong reaction to something, it is likely that it triggered an unconscious memory. See if you can find a past experience that explains your reaction.

Knowing something past is the cause of a current reaction, does not mean it will go away, but it does help you understand why you act the way you do without judging it.

Self-sabotage is normal, it is nature's way of telling you something is wrong in there.

Progress in life is never strictly linear. The unconscious has a way of making sure it isn't. Accept that.

Pain is the result of circumstances, but suffering is what you do to yourself, when you generalize from those circumstances to beliefs about yourself, life and God. All of these things are, in fact, part of life, so they are at worst neutral, not bad. But it doesn't mean you have to believe them.

Remember everyone is doing the best they can. It is better to be honest about your underlying feelings, whether anger, envy, fear, or frustration.

Therapy is well worth doing, but be aware of your expectations (fantasies) about what to expect as far as results. There are deep issues you can overcome, but there may be many you will have to manage or just accept.

SPIRITUALITY

Be aware of signs and "messages" in your environment. Experiment with following them.

Try something (if you haven't already) that develops your "interior awareness," like meditation.

Unsure of whether you should try to change something? Try feeling it out, not just figuring it out.

Break out of routines occasionally to allow synchronicity to work. Trust in your impulses at times and note where they take you.

Choose peaceful environments over stressful ones.

Take time to recharge.

A warning: Beware of spiritual by-passing. Don't let your spiritual attitude prevent you from feeling your emotions or from at times learning life's hard lessons.

NEW AGE

What you are attracting may be a result of subconscious beliefs. Take a look at them.

Don't believe too much of the woo-woo stuff! There's plenty that is helpful, but watch out for fantasy-appeal of some beliefs that can get you hung up on things like DNA restructuring and extra-dimensional beings. Look for things that have some real scientific validation and can actually benefit you and exercise your critical thinking.

MEANING AND PARADOXICAL INTENTION

If you know the *why*, the *how* is more bearable. Can you find some meaning in a situation that is difficult? What would it take, if you knew how, to make the situation more bearable?

Getting through the day (or month or year) is a perfectly good goal when you are depressed. It's better to feel good about doing a little, than feel bad about not doing a lot. Most likely, the world will be fine, whether or not you do something.

Ask yourself: *What is meaningful to me now?*

Ask: *Is there any higher purpose I can find in my circumstances?*
If you feel really bad, try feeling worse.
Try being glad that you are feeling the way you are.

And my personal favorite: Whatever you are thinking, think the opposite. And then back again. For example, it might also look like this: If I do something dumb, I'll think: *I'm glad I did something dumb.* Then, *I hate the fact I did something dumb.* If that hits home, I say, *I'm glad that I hate the fact that I did something dumb.*

MAKE IT YOUR OWN

This list is, of course, incomplete. But even more important, it is only my list. While many of these suggestions may be meaningful for you, every person's psychological structure and experience are different. The purpose in life is to find your own meaning and values, and to structure your life in such a way as to make it work better.

One of the biggest problems with self-help books and seminars is they are a one-size-fits all phenomenon. Obviously, when an author gets a good idea, he or she tries to express it in a simple way, and if the idea is insightful for life, the author can get rather excited about it.

The same thing happened to me. When I had my big breakthrough, I actually thought I had discovered the secret of life. It was so astounding in how it worked and so different from what everyone else was doing that I thought I should write a book about it and charge a thousand dollars a copy. That would have been a great strategy, since the cognitive dissonance theory in psychology shows that in general people value things in direct proportion to how much they pay for them. So by charging that much, I figured I would increase the likelihood of my book being the latest "inside" phenomenon!

But a few months of watching and understanding how my mind works showed me that I was also doing much worth sharing that other people didn't understand. As you know, what works for one person may not work for anyone else. This is because there is much more that someone may be doing than they are not aware of, or that a person may have some background context that makes them unique. This is especially true in regards to self-help books which tend to have the format of case studies or success stories. That's why I have gone into such detail about all aspects of personality in this book.

I approach life with a certain, if you will, *respect*. Every problem is something I puzzle out almost like a chess game. Of course, I am open to messages and synchronicity, but much of the time, I am simply attempting to understand specifically what exactly is going on. Most people don't have the time to spend doing that, which is why I've provided this chapter, giving summaries as a shortcut. But be aware there are times when introspection is needed, as well as unplugging the mind to let answers and synchronicity in.

SOME WISDOM "TO GO"

Pain is part of living—no one can avoid it altogether. How you relate to pain determines whether you become a deep person, as Viktor Frankl's experience pointed out, or a shallow person, or even whether you become an addict to some destructive habit.

I once spoke to a doctor who was the director of a national chain of pain management centers that deal with chronic physical pain, as well as a chain of addiction centers. I was curious about the combination and asked him how he understood the connection, since from what I'd read, people with chronic pain are often addicted to pain killers. Was there some conflict of interest in his two businesses?

The doctor's answer confirmed there was indeed a connection, but not in the way that I had suspected. "I teach people with chronic pain not to expect to eliminate their pain," he told me. "That's what people do when they end up becoming addicted——expect to eliminate the pain completely. Instead, I help them learn to manage the pain."

He explained: "Managing pain means you don't try to eliminate it when buttoning your shirt, but just get the shirt buttoned. A person who can manage their pain is a person who ends up having less of it—and therefore doesn't need to take as many drugs and avoids the risk of becoming addicted."

Satisfied that there was no real contradiction but rather a helpful relationship between his two ventures, I couldn't help but ask him, "Do you think a person can ever be happy when living with chronic pain?" He answered, "Absolutely—but only if they can learn to manage it."

I thought that was a lesson for us all, and a good summary of all that has been discussed. Hopefully, most of us won't have to experience a life of chronic physical pain, but quite a number do experience depression, which is a chronically painful condition in its own right. Learning how to overcome depression is dependent on reaching an understanding about how to deal with emotional pain. Just as the key to managing physical pain is learning how to replace *It hurts when I button my shirt*, with *It hurts but, hey, I buttoned my shirt!*, the key in depression may be trying to feel it doubly or simply in finding words to say, *Today I'm feeling down, but, hey, I am still working towards my meaning* ! (whatever it is.)

So to put all of our research into a final nutshell, here is what we have found: Attempts to control ourselves, whether through Epictetus' advice or positive thinking, are undermined by ironic processes and unconscious sabotage. Fixing unconscious problems is also limited by those problems' deep-seated nature. But interior awareness can lower the stress, paradoxical intention can reduce ironic processes, and meanings and spirituality along with a reminder from Epictetus to accept what we cannot change, can give us enough leverage to manage our direction in a healthy way.

In the end, we can indeed control our feelings about our feelings, and that reduces our suffering which increases our sanity and our chances for happiness.

Finding what works is what used to be called *wisdom*. This exploration is meant to be a starting point. I think Epictetus would agree with the following statement from another ancient source:

> *Wisdom is the principal thing; therefore get wisdom: and with all your getting, get understanding.* (Proverbs 4:7)

The great thing about wanting wisdom is that not only does it help you live your life, but there is no one anywhere that can ever stop you from getting it.

ACKNOWLEDGMENTS

I would like to acknowledge Nancy Marriott for her contribution in organizing and troubleshooting this book. I would also like to thank Peter Mt Shasta, Cynthia Glickman and Ann Scherz for valuable feedback during various drafts. I am also grateful to Denise Buchanan and Richard Caro for putting up with me while I worked through my ideas and used them as sounding boards, as well as people like Dr. Thomas Scheff, Bart Clouston, and Ron Levy who gave me food for thought and core ideas that sprouted much later though sometimes in unexpected ways. Finally, thanks to all my friends who repeatedly told me "You should write a book," when I sprang on them some odd piece of advice or apparent insight.

APPENDIX

RECOMMENDED READING, CHAPTER ENDNOTES, AND FURTHER REFERENCES

RECOMMENDED READING, ENDNOTES AND FURTHER REFERENCES BY CHAPTER

CHAPTER ONE: THOUGHTS, FEELINGS, AND HAPPINESS

Recommended Reading:

Barbara Ehrenreich, *Bright-Sided: How Positive Thinking Is Undermining America*. MacMillan, 2010

Sharon Lebell, *The Art of Living: The Classic Manual on Virtue, Happiness, and Effectiveness*. HarperCollins, 2004

Daniel M. Wegner, *White Bears and Other Unwanted Thoughts: Suppression, Obsession, and the Psychology of Mental Control*. Guilford Press, 1994.

Endnotes:

1. The *Encyclopedia of Philosophy* by Donald M. Borchert (Editor) was first published in 1967 and updated in 2005. The first edition was published in eight large volumes in 1967.
2. Todd Kashdan, "The Problem with Happiness." Huffington Post. Sept 30, 2010 (online version)

3. Joanne Wood, *et al.* "Positive Self-Statements: Power for Some, Peril for Others." *Psychological Science.* July 2009, Vol. 20, No. 7, pp. 860-866.
4. Lisa Miller from "Huston Smith's Wonderful Life." *Newsweek.* May 1, 2009 (online version)
5. Myriam Mongrain and Susan Sergeant, As cited in Jennifer Abassi's article "Positive Psychology: How to Use it Wisely." IVillage.com, Dec 13, 2011 (online version)
6. Elizabeth Carter wrote *All the Works of Epictetus, Which are Now Extant* in 1758. Excerpts are from Wikiquotes.

Further References:
Alan Watts, *The Meaning of Happiness: The Quest for Freedom of the Spirit in Modern Psychology and the Wisdom of the East.* Harper and Row, 1970

CHAPTER TWO: RE-THINKING HAPPINESS ... AND UNHAPPINESS

Recommended Reading:
Robert Heilbroner, *An Inquiry Into the Human Prospect.* Norton, 1991
Gregory David Roberts, *Shantaram: A Novel.* St Martin's Press, 2003

Endnotes:
1. *Publisher's Weekly* Editorial Review of Marci Shimoff's *Happy for No Reason.* (Online at Amazon.com)
2. Jonah Lehrer, "Depression's Upside." *New York Times*, February 25, 2010 (online version)
3. Daniel Carlat, "Mind Over Meds." *New York Times*, April 23, 2010 (online version)
4. Freider R. Lang et al, "Forecasting Life Satisfaction Across Adulthood: Benefits of Seeing a Darker Future," *Psychology and Aging*, 2013: Vol 10:1037

Further References:
Richard Carlson, *Don't Sweat the Small Stuff and It's All Small Stuff*. Hyperion, 1996
Eckhart Tolle, *The Power of Now: A Guide to Spiritual Enlightenment*. New World Library, 1999
Marci Shimoff, *Happy for No Reason: Seven Steps to Being Happy From the Inside Out*. Simon and Shuster, 2008

CHAPTER THREE: THE MOTION OF EMOTIONS

Recommended Reading:
Gordon Clanton, Lynn G. Smith. *Jealousy*. Prentice-Hall, 1998
Daniel Goleman, *Emotional Intelligence, 10th Anniversary Edition*. Random House, 2012
Daniel M. Wegner, *The Illusion of Conscious Will*. MIT Press, 2003

Endnotes:
1. Richard Stevens, et al. "Swearing as a Response to Pain." *Neuroreport:* 5 August 2009, Volume 20, Issue 12, pp. 1056-1060.

Further References:
Thomas Scheff, *Microsociology: Discourse, Emotion, and Social Structure*. University of Chicago, 1994
Ernest Hartmann, *Boundaries in the Mind: A New Psychology of Personality*. Basic Books, 1991
Harvey Jackins, *The Human Side of Human Beings: The Theory of Re-evaluation Counseling*. Seattle, WA. Rational Island Publications, 1978

CHAPTER FOUR: THE UNCONSCIOUS MIND

Recommended Reading:
Sigmund Freud, *The Interpretation of Dreams*. London, Megadolon, 2010 (Originally 1899)

Endnotes:
1. More can be found about the history of hypnosis at Bryn Mawr University's *Serendip* website: http://serendip.brynmawr.edu/Mind/Trance.html
2. More about Freud's patient Dora in *Dora: An Analysis of a Case of Hysteria* by Sigmund Freud, Simon & Schuster, 1905.

CHAPTER FIVE: A SPIRITUAL JOURNEY TO THE EAST

Recommended Reading:
Carl Jung, *Memories, Dreams, Reflections*. Random House, 1989 (Originally 1961)
Peter Mt Shasta, *Adventures of a Western Mystic: Apprentice to the Masters*. Author House, 2010
Pete A. Sanders, *You Are Psychic! The Free Soul Method*. Simon & Schuster, 1999
Ian Stevenson, *Children Who Remember Past Lives. A Question of Reincarnation*. Jefferson, NC. McFarland Publications, 2001

Endnotes:
1. For more on *interior awareness*, see Emma Seppala, "Decoding The Body Watcher." *Scientific American*. April 3, 2012 (on-line Version)
2. For more on Husserl, see Dermot Moran, *Edmund Husserl: Founder Phenomenology*. Cambridge, UK. Polity Press, 2005
3. Princeton University study of money and happiness, see: http://www.time.com/time/magazine/article/0,9171,2019628,00.html

Further References:

Benjamin Barber, *Jihad vs. McWorld: Terrorism's Challenge to Democracy*. Crown, 1995

Hermann Hesse, *Journey to the East* (translator: Hilda Rosner) Picador; Reprint edition, 2003

Jack Kornfield, *A Path with Heart: A Guide Through the Perils and Promises of Spiritual Life*. Bantam, 1993

Rodney Stark and William Sims Bainbridge, *The Future of Religion: Secularization, Revival and Cult Formation*. University of California Press, 1985

Clifford Geertz, *Islam Observed: Religious Development in Morocco and Indonesia*, Yale University Press, 1968

Richard Wilhelm (Translator), Cary F. Baynes (Translator), C. G. Jung (Foreword), *The I Ching or Book of Changes*. Princeton University Press; 3rd edition, 1967

CHAPTER SIX: THE NEW AGE

Endnotes:

1. For more on the Gaia Hypthesis, see: James Lovelock, *Gaia: A New Look at Life on Earth* (3rd ed.). Oxford University Press, 2000 [1979]
2. For more on the UCLA experiments of Harold Garfinkle, see: Garfinkel, H. "Common sense knowledge of social structures: The documentary method of interpretation in lay and professional fact finding." In H. Garfinkel (Ed.), *Studies in Ethnomethodology*. Prentice-Hall, 1967
3. Ron Suskind, *The One Percent Doctrine: Deep inside America's Pursuit of Enemies Since 9/11*. Simon & Schuster, 2006.
4. William Wells cited in Jennifer Abassi, "Positive Psychology: How to Use it Wisely." IVillage.com Dec 13, 2011 (online version)

Further References:
Rhonda Byrne, *The Secret*. Atria Books, 2006
Henri Ellenberger, *The Discovery Of The Unconscious: The History And Evolution Of Dynamic Psychiatry*. Basic Books, 1970
Kahlil Gibran is quoted from his book, *The Prophet*. Knopf, 1973
Malcolm Maltz, *Psycho-Cybernetics*. Prentice-Hall, 1960
Padma Sambhava, Robert Thurman, The Dalai Lama and Karma Lingpa, *The Tibetan Book of the Dead: The Great Book of Natural Liberation Through Understanding in the Between*. Bantam, 1993
Daniel M. Wegner, *The Illusion of Conscious Will*. MIT Press, 2002

CHAPTER SEVEN: THE MEANING OF LIFE

Recommended Reading:
Petrūska Clarkson and Jennifer MacKewn, *Fritz Perls*. Sage Publications, 1993
James C. Collins, *Good to Great*. London. William Collins Co., 2001
Viktor Frankl, *Man's Search for Meaning*. Simon & Schuster, 1997 (Originally 1959)
Viktor Frankl, *The Doctor and the Soul. An Introduction to Logotherapy*. A. Knopf, 1962

Further References:
Gordon Allport, *The Individual and His Religion: A Psychological Interpretation* Macmillan, 1957

ABOUT THE AUTHOR

Dr. Robert Manis is currently Professor of Human Behavior at the College of Southern Nevada. Dr. Manis has published three books: *The Marriage and Family Workbook* (Allyn and Bacon, 2000), *Challenge to Society* (Pearson, 2001) and *The Social Reality,* (Sage/Hall Communications, 2005).

www.ingramcontent.com/pod-product-compliance
Lightning Source LLC
Chambersburg PA
CBHW030320080526
44584CB00012B/648